Unravelled
Contemporary Knit Art

Unravelled
Contemporary Knit Art

Charlotte Vannier

With over 400 illustrations

 Thames & Hudson

CONTENTS

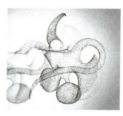

INTRODUCTION

The crafts of knitting and crochet have long been regarded as forms of folk art. Created from a single length of yarn, using knitting needles or a crochet hook to form interconnected loops, knitted fabrics are primarily used to make warm clothing and other domestic items, and they implicitly evoke the notions of protection, love and maternal care.

Still predominantly associated with female makers, knitting and crochet are key parts of the domestic history of women, who may have practised these crafts as an economic necessity or as a useful pastime. Generations of women have not only passed on their knowledge and skills but also the satisfaction of working by hand with passion and patience. Nowadays, in an era when industrialization and the concepts of business and profitability are at odds with the simplicity and rustic nature of handicrafts, these ancient skills still retain an aura of nostalgia. But by taking up practices regarded as dated and irrevocably bound up with old-fashioned imagery, contemporary artists are now deliberately breaking these traditional codes. They are being inspired to rediscover, invent and reinvent, utilizing a process that creates structure in order to deconstruct and reconstruct.

The slow pace of knitting and crochet is another source of attraction for artists, forcing them to build up their works stitch by stitch, enraptured by the time-consuming yet meditative aspects of a craft for which they must slow down their brains to match the speed of their hands. Once the stereotypical views of yarnwork as outdated and subservient have been set aside, a new and liberating sculptural potential comes to light. The lengthy creative process teaches artists patience and humility, often making their fingers and arms ache, sometimes sending them into a kind of trance.

Whether tiny or huge, multicoloured or monochrome, abstract or realistic, intimate or exhibitionist, knitted works are now invading galleries, museums and public spaces. Knitting and crochet have become a means of artistic expression as valid as drawing, painting, sculpture and photography. Simple and accessible materials such as wool, acrylic, cotton, wire, and rope can be used to fashion works of art that are unique, modern, challenging or even disturbing, making spectators reconsider the objects and beliefs that fill their day-to-day lives.

By showcasing forty artists who incorporate knitting, crochet and felting into their practice, this book seeks to provide an overview of yarnwork in contemporary art, demonstrating how and why each maker has chosen these techniques as a form of expression.

Knitting and crochet give these artists direction and add meaning to their creations. For Aurélie Mathigot, they become a kind of protective membrane that envelops the objects and their maker. Dimitri Tsykalov uses them to echo the demands of our consumerist society. For Nathan Vincent, they reflect issues of gender, while for Casey Jenkins, they raise the concerns of feminism. Jo Hamilton wants to rehabilitate the contemporary image of crafts by creating figurative art. Ben Cuevas sees them as political and metaphysical, inspired by concepts of feminity, pop culture and the human mind and body. Often associated with the ideas of memory and tradition, these techniques do not merely send out a political or poetic message, but moreover invite a kind of intimacy and proximity, while at the same time proving that works created with needles can become genuine works of art.

From New York to Berlin, Melbourne to the Faroe Islands, Saarbrücken to Utrecht, Lisbon to Paris, a new kind of art is being woven from yarn, growing steadily stitch by stitch, and making a variety of statements, whether subtle or bold, ironic or sublime.

Charlotte Vannier

KATE JENKINS

PLACE OF RESIDENCE
BRIGHTON, UK

PLACE OF BIRTH
NEWPORT, UK

DATE OF BIRTH
1971

WEBSITE
**KATEJENKINSSTUDIO.
CO.UK**

Kate Jenkins takes a nostalgic look at ordinary objects and reinvents them in wool, infusing them with a dash of wit, warmth and poetry. A graduate in fashion and textiles, she has worked as a knitwear designer with several famous labels and designers in the UK and elsewhere. In the lively town of Brighton, a popular tourist destination, Kate crochets in a studio that doubles as a shop. She uses fine crochet hooks, usually 1.5 or 1.75 mm, and only works with lambswool, creating cans of sardines, plates of fish and chips, tins of catfood, red mullets with shimmering scales, prawns, doughnuts, stuffed packets of Woolboro cigarettes, bottles of Katez Tomato Stitchup, tins of Campbell's Crocheted Tomato Soup, bottles of Veuve Tricot, and more.

Influenced by everything around her, Kate reconstructs everyday items in crochet. She concentrates on things that bring a smile to her face, using this as the point of departure for her creative process. Always on the look-out for new ideas, she travels from country to country to absorb other cultures.

Without claiming an affiliation with any particular art movement, she has an unconditional love of embroidery and is strongly inspired by the designs of Paul Poiret and his friend and follower Elsa Schiaparelli.

Above:
Sequined King Prawns
(detail), installation at
Alexandra Palace, 2015

Right:
*Hand Sewn
Seafood*, created
for Viking Cruises;
machine-knitted and
hand-embroidered
seafood, 2016

Kate Jenkins 2016

Right:
Tinned Lobster Bisque
35 × 52.5 cm
Machine-knitted lobster
with hand-embroidered
sequins, in a lobster
can, 2017

Opposite, below left:
Sardines and Lobster
(detail), installation at
Alexandra Palace, 2015

Above and below:
Tinned Pilchards
33 × 52.5 cm
Machine-knitted pilchards
hand-embroidered with
sequins, 2017

Above:
Sardines on Toast
Machine-knitted and
sewn sardines on hand-
crocheted toast, 2014

Together, those two designers seem to her to reflect an ideal combination of technique, beauty, wit and surrealism, creating works of art in the form of fashion.

Kate first began to crochet at the age of fifteen, taught by her mother who was a prolific crochet artist and crafter, and then became fascinated with the crochet hook, attracted by its speed of movement and simplicity. She has given up working with viscose and silk in favour of lambswool, which she finds easy to handle.

Whether she is designing a piece of clothing or a 3D crocheted object, she uses the same technique, the same stitches and the same kind of yarn, fascinated by the idea of using an identical process on different media or materials. She says she finds crocheting therapeutic and good for the heart and mind, and that she is driven by the need to crochet something new as soon as she has finished any given project. When halfway through a piece, she is galvanized by the way it

Above:
*Smoked Salmon and
Scrambled Eggs on Toast*
Machine-knitted smoked salmon,
hand-crocheted scrambled
eggs, toast and lemon, 2015

Opposite:
Squid in Ink
Machine-knitted squid,
hand-embroidered with
sequins, 2015

'Ever since I was a child, I've loved the method of creating something 3D out of a ball of wool and a hook.'

Above:
*Assorted Sewshi
with Sew Sauce*
Crocheted and hand-
embroidered sushi, 2011

gradually begins to take form and starts to resemble the idea she had at the outset. Her favourite of all her pieces – a fish counter, exhibited in London and Dublin in 2015 – had been gestating for years. It took nine months for her to crochet the huge range of fish and shellfish that populate this glittering display. She is often asked to collaborate

with other artists, including Jon Link and Mick Bunnage, the writers, cartoonists and animators of the satirical cult comic *Modern Toss*, for whom she designed the Knitted Alan Action Figure. Kate has also reworked products for brands such as Pommery champagne, Liberty of London, and Dine cat food.

Above:
*Smoked Salmon
and Cream Cheese
Poppy Seed Bagel*
Hand-crocheted and
embroidered, 2012

SOLÈNE
LEBON-COUTURIER

PLACE OF RESIDENCE
PARIS

PLACE OF BIRTH
LÉHON, FRANCE

DATE OF BIRTH **1981**

WEBSITE
**BEHANCE.NET/
LEBON-COUTURIER**

Solène Lebon-Couturier loves to explore the link between illustration and knitting and engage playfully with the borderline between art and crafts. She pays tribute to the people who have had an impact on her by knitting images of them: 'Their story and their talents call out to me and what they give me back inspires me to interpret them in knitted form.'

After studying Spanish in Rennes and then gaining a teaching qualification in 2005, she rediscovered the craft of knitting that she first learned from her grandmothers and aunts when she was five years old, while continuing to work as a teacher. She was inspired by

Michel Gondry's film *The Science of Sleep*, in which Charlotte Gains-bourg and Gael García Bernal dream up strange and poetic knitted objects. From then on, her ideas began to develop, starting with a series of dolls: Michael Jackson, Marilyn Monroe, the stars of *Sex and the City*, Marie Antoinette and even Karl Lagerfeld. Solène dropped off the Lagerfeld doll one day at the Chanel reception desk, only to see him much later, sitting on the lap of Cara Delevingne in an ad campaign for the autumn/winter 2013–14 Chanel collection.

She has gone on to produce knitted street art and create various installations with the Collectif France Tricot, a collective she co-founded in 2008 after meeting two other women who shared her passion via social media: Céline Lacome-Hulin and Emmanuelle

Above and opposite:
The Stripper, after
Cédric Bucaille
Each panel 23 × 43 cm
Wool, intarsia, 2014

Barrère (see p. 176). Together they began to explore yarn bombing, a form of knitted street art that had just begun to cross the Atlantic, with the aim of inspiring a softer form of graffiti. Now, inspired by the pared-down graphic art of illustrators like René Gruau and Malika Favre and films such as *Carrie*, *The Shining*, *Jaws* and *Pierrot le Fou*, Solène focuses on illustration work and knitted portraits.

She always remains aware of the sense of touch and movement involved in knitting, and loves the medium because it is soft and warm and because of its colourful palette and simplicity. The mean-dering process calls for a slow pace and allows the knitter to do

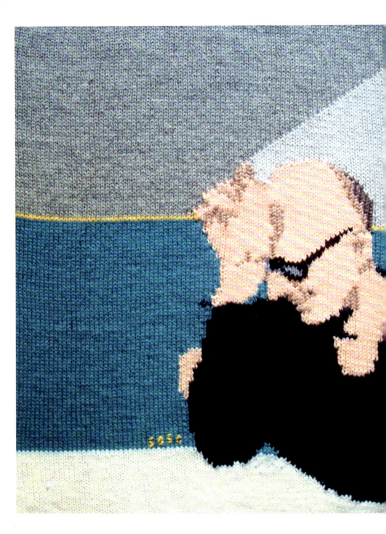

something else at the same time, like watching a good film – or a bad one: 'I like working slowly, but I'm always short of time.'

The pixel-like stitches form a two- or three-dimensional work, creating an interplay of textures and caressing the eye with their unusual warmth and slight imperfections. Solène works out of a desire to turn the images in her mind into reality, while maintaining the momentum of the moment: 'If I don't do it at once, I won't do it at all.' She generally uses 3.5 mm needles and yarn made of natural fibres in plain, bold colours, preferring ethical and sustainable wools, along with organic and cruelty-free dyes. Solène lets

Above:
Bike, after Cédric Bucaille
40 × 40 cm
Wool, intarsia and
embroidery, 2014

herself be carried away by the thrill of creating an image, eager for the moment when the results become visible, as in the case of *Bather With Chrysanthemums* (opposite), a work of which she is very proud: 'It was a constraint to work with fresh flowers. I loved seeing how the knitting came together with the flowers and the installation gradually took shape.'

'People often tell me: "This is the first time I've ever seen knitted illustrations." I don't believe I belong to any movement. Does textile illustration count as one?'

Bather With Chrysanthemums Knitted wool and cotton, bath, fresh flowers, 2014

LILI BEL

PLACE OF RESIDENCE
MONTREUIL, FRANCE

PLACE OF BIRTH
CANNES, FRANCE

DATE OF BIRTH **1967**

WEBSITE
LILI-BEL.COM

Member of the collective
Fiber Art Fever! since
its founding in 2010

Lili Bel is concerned first and foremost with human relationships, especially romantic ones. A compulsive maker, hardworking, perfectionist and dedicated, she is proud to be a woman and fights to find her place in a society she sees as chauvinist and often unfair.

At the age of twenty-five, after three years at the ESAA Duperré college in Paris, then another three at the School of Decorative Arts, Lili started a family and began to work as an artist. She earned a living by teaching the applied arts for some ten years, then moved towards film set design as a painter.

At the School of Decorative Arts she attended a course on 'urban experiments' taught by the writer and drama critic René Gady and the architect Yves Tissier. The students were required to use their

Above left:
Delights of Spring
680 × 350 cm
Crochet, wool, 2011

Above:
Vertiginous
Prevarications
260 × 410 cm
Crochet, wool, 2016

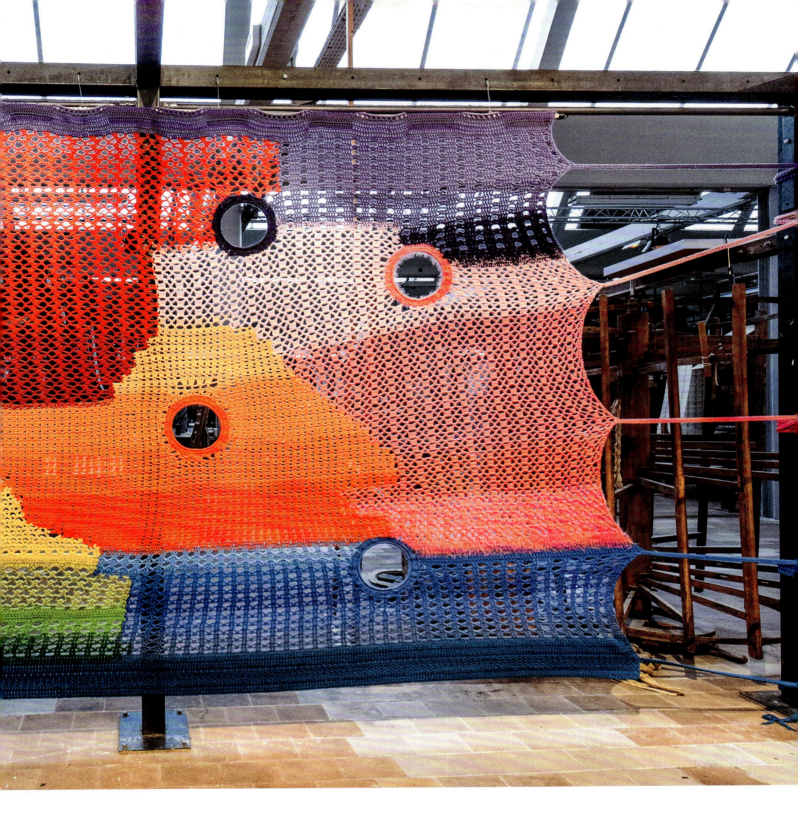

bodies, voices and any other medium they could imagine, and treat their subject as a kind of performance acted out in the form of their choosing: photography, video, sound or text. This unusual evening class proved a revelation to Lili. It was where she discovered powerful artists such as Sophie Calle and Jean-Pierre Raynaud: 'I can say that I became what I am at the end of that course.' She realized that her life could be turned into a theatre of her own design: 'Life itself could be

a source of inspiration.' From then on, her training as an artist and set designer began to feed her interest in spaces.

Her sources of inspiration are very diverse: a piece of work may be inspired by a novel, or perhaps just a phrase or sentence that speaks to her and which she notes in her workbook for later use, or maybe an object unearthed in a flea market or yard sale. But she also responds to calls for projects on specific subjects, always thinking up new

Above:
Head in the Stars
410 × 110 cm
(hopscotch ladder);
22 × 17 cm
(7 surrounding pieces)
Crocheted wool,
embroidery thread,
graph paper,
pebbles, 2008

ways of turning them into reality. Everyday life is also a major source of inspiration: 'I try to highlight the experiences of life. The ones that repeat themselves.' She deals with difficult events by utilizing the emotions they evoke: 'It is a kind of therapy.' Life in general inspires her, especially love and dis-enchantment. Her work is often autobiographical, recalling the art of Annette Messager and Sophie Calle.

In 1999, while assembling small works she calls 'memory boxes', she first decided to include wool in her art. For a piece called *Turn Off That TV!* she collected small squares of wool knitted by an old lady she knew, put them all together and crocheted a border to create a table mat for a television to stand on. In her *Memories of Childhood* (2000–1) series, she incorporated threads of stretched yarn. It was in 2004, however, that wool and the technique of crochet became her favourite medium and she produced her first large-format piece, entitled *A Spider on the Ceiling* (p. 31); it took her a year to complete and, at the time, seemed immense to her. Nevertheless, she has gone on to create several larger works, including the biggest so far, *Delights of Spring* (2011; p. 24), measuring 24 m² and completed in just a few months.

She finds crocheting to be a soothingly repetitive task. As she works, she feels a sense of serenity and release, finding herself in a blissful, almost meditative state. She regards the slow pace of the technique as a

Opposite above:
Overflow
12 elements, each
c. 23.5 × 35.5 cm
Crochet, wool,
photographs
© Paco, 2016

Opposite below:
Overflow 08
35 × 35.5 cm
Crochet, wool,
photographs
© Paco, 2016

Above:
The Thread of My Intertwined Thoughts
250 × 200 × 200 cm
Stretched and woven woollen yarn,
wooden frame, 2016

The Thread of My Encircling Thoughts
Diameter 700 cm
Crocheted woollen rug, 2014

necessary part of her creative process: 'My idea is developed stitch by stitch and the work takes shape'. Crocheting frees her hand and her arm; the movements are loose and the technique satisfying, despite its slowness. It is so flexible that it opens up a number of possibilities and means that a piece can be transformed as she is making it. She

Below:
*The Thread of My Intertwined
Thoughts* (maquette)
Stretched and woven woollen
yarn, metal frame, 2016

Bottom:
Reprise!
exhibition (detail),
La Manufacture
Roubaix, France, 2016

always looks at the work as a whole: 'I may begin a piece row by row, then continue by going round it. Stop using one method and juxtapose another. Form a hole then change stitch.' For each new piece, she discovers new tricks and new stitches to try out, even if she has sketched out the overall shape from the start: 'The fact of changing the process, of modifying the data, opens it all up in an incredibly satisfying way.' Wool fascinates Lili and offers her a painterly palette of colours with countless shades. To start out with a yarn and then form a flat surface is a process she finds magical every time. She primarily works with bright, stimulating and complementary colours, which

29

Above:
It's All Over (detail)
120 × 160 cm,
29 × 32 cm (8 pieces)
Crocheted wool,
embroidery thread,
stiffened muslin,
metal chains, 2012

light up the dullness of everyday life, like beams of energy coursing through her studio. Working in close contact with her material is a source of comfort and she enjoys its softness. She varies the thickness of the yarn – sometimes also using sewing thread to give her woven pieces a little more tension and make them less elastic – and combines a huge variety of different textures. Lili not only crochets in wool but also uses string, fabric, plastic, old video tape and even hair to form stitches, preferring to use a 7 mm crochet hook, or a 12 mm hook for larger works. For medium- and large-format pieces, she combines crochet with other techniques, including embroidery, photography, or both. Experimental, with a fairly simple vocabulary, her crochet pieces often feature effects that recall woven fabrics and lace.

Lili Bel's creations are born of a driving need to make, and by the pleasure of communicating about subjects she cares about, and of expressing herself through this medium, in a way that always reflects the passage of time. The more difficult a piece is to complete, the happier she is, and she likes to work on an ambitious scale. Sometimes she includes words in her art; at other times her works engage with the space around them. Yet her approach is very spontaneous, driven by what she calls 'revelations', ideas to which she is eager to give form, desires she finds it impossible to ignore. The journey from

the initial concept to the act of creation then becomes an absolute necessity to her. Her art often includes a conceptual aspect too, since her knowledge of art history has always helped her to keep following her own particular approach: 'It is often a question of bringing together ideas, facts and techniques that are germinating in my mind, which is always on the look-out for something new.'

Left and above:
A Spider on the Ceiling
H. 172 cm, diam. 80 cm
Crocheted wool,
embroidery thread,
stiffened muslin, pins,
photo prints, metal,
2005–8

KATHARINA
KRENKEL

PLACE OF RESIDENCE
**SAARBRÜCKEN,
GERMANY**

PLACE OF BIRTH
**BUENOS AIRES,
ARGENTINA**

DATE OF BIRTH
1966

WEBSITE
**KATHARINA-KRENKEL.
DE**

Pragmatic, from a hardworking German Protestant background, Katharina Krenkel crochets in a state of contemplation and calm. Her sculptures are soft and washable.

She first began to knit one day while sitting on the corner of a sofa with a bag of old scraps of wool and soon discovered that she could crochet anything she wished, big or small, sweet or strange, and started to use this historically feminine craft to explore themes from everyday life. Because it is such an easy technique to master, she finds that she can crochet her works anywhere, in any situation, at any time.

She studied at the University of Arts in Saarbrücken, which at the time was a new institution that encouraged an interdisciplinary approach and taught design, painting, drawing and performance art. During her first year of studies, one of her teachers, Oskar Holweck,

who taught the basics of composition according to Bauhaus principles, became one of her major influences. His teaching principles focused mainly on chiaroscuro, colour, form and structure, rhythm and space. But her most important inspiration has always been O.W. Himmel, her artistic associate, with whom she has lived, worked and studied for a long time. She is also influenced by Louise Bourgeois, Annette Messager, Wiebke Siem and Yayoi Kusama, as well as by the soft sculptures of Claes Oldenburg. As a sculptor who has chosen crochet as her medium and yarn as her material, she does not claim to belong to any movement except her own, which she defines as 'slow art'.

Her studio is a small wooden shed set in a huge garden. She draws her inspiration from nature, everyday life and society, which she

Above:
Vermin
7 pieces, each
c. 100 × 30 × 30 cm
Yarn, crochet,
painting, 2013

Opposite:
Matrix
40 × 40 cm, 60 ×
60 cm, 90 × 90 cm,
130 × 130 cm; ball:
30 × 30 × 30 cm
Rubber, crochet, 4 flat
pieces, 1 ball, 2015

Left and opposite:
*Lace Underpants/
Inside and Outside*
65 × 65 × 55 cm
Knitted and
crocheted cotton,
rose thorns, steel
hoops, 2016

observes from a distance: 'I transform the most boring chores, like folding the washing, into forms of research for my art.'

She began to crochet in 1993, using all kinds of materials as her yarn: leftover odds and ends, old reels of yarn dating back to the 1970s, scraps of rubber from the motor industry, bits of tape, wire, and more. Preferring drawing to painting, she thinks in terms of line rather than surface and crochets three-dimensional designs, layering the stitches on top of each other like elements in space.

An image, a small sketch or a new material can suddenly catch her attention and set her off crocheting for hours, using hooks of all sizes, her fingers, or even tools she fashions herself. Comfortably settled in her favourite 'crochet' chair, Katharina creates a body of work full of unusual and unexpected images. At the back of her mind lies the constant fear that she will not have enough time to bring all the creatures of her dreams to life: 'Unfortunately my fingers do not move as fast as my brain.' She particularly savours the moment when the end of the process is approaching and the almost-completed piece is lying on her knees and keeping her warm. The flexibility of her sculptures makes them easy to transport and store. Their empty, balloon-like forms can be filled with newspaper, whose ink is a deterrent to moths that might otherwise nibble on them: 'I dream of an exhibition that can be stored in a single suitcase.'

For her installation *SOS – Save Our Souls* (opposite), probably the work that has given her most satisfaction, she crocheted 49 starched lace lifebelts, of different sizes and with different motifs: 'I have never managed to keep the lifebelts immaculate and in their original shape.' When they are hung in situ, they soon become yellow and fade, as a result of the light and humidity: 'Perhaps it was arrogant to imagine I could represent and save souls. But my own practice taught me I could and proved it.'

The crocheted *Skull* (above right), although designed originally to be used as a calling card, has become another key work in Katharina's oeuvre. To demonstrate how serious her intentions were in regard to crochet, and to prove to people she met at parties that she is neither an artist who paints nor an artist who crochets but a sculptor, she had postcards printed with images of the skull, accompanied by the phrase: 'Crochet is damn serious business.'

DIMITRI TSYKALOV

PLACE OF RESIDENCE
PARIS

PLACE OF BIRTH
MOSCOW, RUSSIA

DATE OF BIRTH **1963**

WEBSITE
DIMITRITSYKALOV.COM

Dimitri Tsykalov studied graphic art at Moscow Polygraphic Institute while also studying drawing and painting in the studio of Moscow painters Leonid Lamm and A. Zhilikov. As a young graduate, he settled in Paris in 1991 and received a special prize for young painters in 1999. An artist in every sense, he uses a variety of techniques, from painting and drawing to installations, photography and sculpture, as well as knitting.

In April 2000, the NASDAQ index collapsed, an event that had repercussions on stock markets around the world. In Paris, CAC 40 began to drop in December 2000 (later accentuated by the September 11 terrorist attacks in 2001) and this did not end until March 2003 when the

Above:
Bank of America 6411
87 × 160 cm
Wool, 2009

Opposite:
Money exhibition,
Galerie Rabouan
Moussion, Paris, 2009

index recorded a fall of 65%. In 2005, as the world was still recovering from that disaster and no one was expecting another catastrophe to come along, Dimitri began a new work, *Money*. It was a sad premonition of the international financial crash and the collapse of the world economy that was to follow a few years later. *Money* was born very quietly, from an armada of Russian, Polish and Hungarian craftspeople knitting away, like Penelope, at oversized multicoloured credit cards that Dimitri has designed, representing a variety of banks. These little plastic cards, iconic yet ridiculous, even tyrannical, now took on a different dimension, whether symbolically or simply

because of their huge size (around 150 cm across). *Disney Chase*, *Hello Kitty Chase*, *Seven Royal* (a card granting the right to $100,000 of credit, reserved for the lucky few whose monthly credit line reaches a total of $200 million), *UBS Mastercard* (issued by the largest wealth-management bank in the world), *Bank of Rajasthan* (with India moving towards becoming the third largest economic power in the world): the artist produced 14 knitted credit cards in total and hung them in space. Deliberately left unfinished and still attached to a ball of wool left lying on the floor, they make us question the needs of our consumer society. The cards were accompanied by an immaculate *Cash Machine* (opposite), created from openwork lace.

A year before *Money*, Dimitri created *Plantation à la Carte*, a series of photographs showing himself planting a bank card and hoping it will grow, come wind or snow. These photographs were followed by an installation at the Salomon de Rothschild Foundation in

Paris, which took the form of a flowerbed, measuring 6 metres by 10 metres, representing a Crédit Agricole credit card in full bloom.

Art can be a form of catharsis or release, but Dimitri uses it to highlight the violence that runs rampant in modern society. He does this not only through knitting, but also through the use of fragile, ephemeral or living materials. Whether made of wood (*Woodlands*), meat (*Meat*, *Body* and *Masks*), fruit and vegetables (*Skulls* and *Body*) or wool (*Money*), his sculptures disturb, question and teach us, through a skilful mix of brutality and poetry, to remain aware of the fleeting nature of life, the fury of war and its trail of death, terrorism and weaponry, and also to make fun of our world. This use of non-traditional materials seems to be a way of persuading us to pay closer attention.

Dimitri Tsykalov exhibits regularly at the Galerie Rabouan Moussion in Paris.

Above left:
Eurasian Bank Diamond 4066
86 × 157 cm
Wool, 2009

Above right:
Cash Machine
85 × 45 cm
Wool, 2009

Below left:
Amex Black 3766
45 × 98 cm
Wool, 2009

AGNÈS SÉBYLEAU

PLACE OF RESIDENCE
CHARENTON-LE-PONT, FRANCE

PLACE OF BIRTH
VALENCE, FRANCE

DATE OF BIRTH **1961**

WEBSITE
SEBYLEAU.ULTRA-BOOK. COM

In 2009, Agnès Sébyleau was working as an art director at an ad agency when she first picked up a crochet hook and felt an intense sense of joy: 'All sorts of possibilities came into my head.' So she gave up working with pixels and embraced crochet, finding an unexpected parallel between the two. Since then, without having any particular masterplan in mind, she has followed her own creative path. She uses nothing but twine, usually untreated (never animal fibre), to

make her fabric. Usually it is linen and, more recently, hemp, which is even more rustic and dense, allowing her to create more solid works. Flexible enough to be crocheted yet tough enough to add rigidity, cheap and easy to source, twine allows her to shape her works very freely. She lets its pale colour, rather like that of wood, be her guide and adds colour as a kind of punctuation: 'What interests me

Above, from left to right:
Celestine
30 × 38 × 10 cm
Crocheted from a single length of hemp twine, 2016

Shooting Star
51 × 37 × 12 cm
Crocheted hemp and linen twine, 2016

Autofictive Locomotion
90 × 30 × 16 cm
Crocheted from a single length of hemp twine, 2014

Opposite:
Vertico
100 × 70 × 40 cm (7 pieces)
Crocheted from a single length of linen twine, 2015

is the adventure of form. Developing a form, playing with empty spaces, delving into the shadows, showing the ebb and flow.' She sources her raw twine in DIY stores, and her white or red twine in a kitchenware shop: it's butcher's twine used mainly for roasts and sausages: 'Haberdashery is not my world.'

Agnès likes the unassuming nature of crochet and its apparently endless possibilities. It certainly takes a long time and is repetitive but it can be done anywhere, and quite discreetly: the simplicity of the tools and materials contrasts with their huge creative potential: 'There is no doubt a certain pride in doing so much with so little.'

The only disadvantage of crochet, to the artist's mind, is that it's often associated with the world of 'feminine' hobbies and isn't given the same consideration as other artistic media: 'It's always being misunderstood.'

Agnès describes her technique as rudimentary: 'I crochet badly, I hold my hook badly and I hold my yarn badly.' She is not a crochet artist in the purest sense: the hook is purely a tool to her and she is not interested in technique. Nor is she trying to create pretty pieces. Her works are basic: free and untamed, they reflect her unique creative approach and they grow naturally out of the material she uses: 'As for the rest, I get by, I find solutions.' Using a 4 mm hook like an extension of her body, she finds the yarn makes its own demands that feed into her work. As a material, it is flexible yet rigid enough to allow the shapes to expand indefinitely and to let her create a balance between volumes and flatter areas. She has to cope with the variations in thickness and the slight twisting of the twine caused by it being wound around the bobbin: 'The fabric I create has a mineral

Above:
The Line
Set of 6 pieces
Crocheted linen with
synthetic stuffing, 2016

quality. Alternatively, it is a stretched skin, sometimes inert and sometimes sensitive. By accepting its irregularities I allow it to move. For someone as rigid as I am, it's enriching.' When the piece begins to look something like what was originally in her mind, the artist tells herself: 'So this is what it's going to look like.' She sees this as the most important stage in the process and is often surprised, sometimes disappointed, occasionally delighted. Her pieces take shape silently, spontaneously, without the help of sketches. She makes no notes, simply following the rhythm of the growing work, captivated by the journey the yarn is taking.

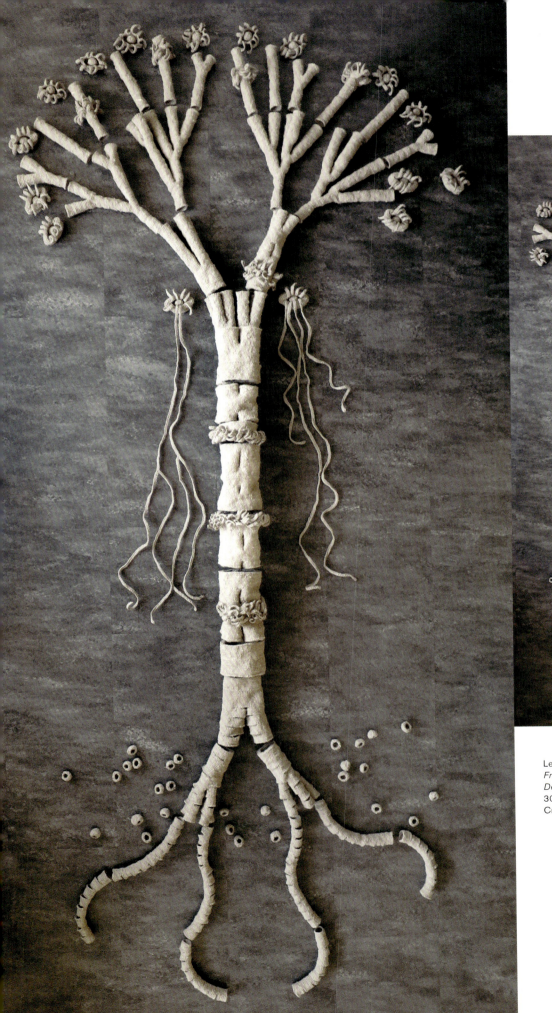

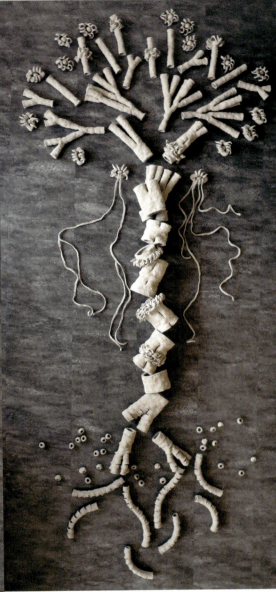

Left and above:
*Fragments in a
Devastated Garden*
300 × 150 × 20 cm
Crocheted hemp, 2017

Above:
Fear of the Void
51 × 19 × 17 cm
Crocheted from a single
length of linen twine, 2014

Left:
I Miss You
66 × 28 × 20 cm
Crocheted linen, paint
and wire, 2013

Agnès describes her work as meticulous but also austere. She likes it to remain crude, raw and restrained, and distrusts prettiness and charm, although she does like to add a touch of wit and playfulness. Although they are neither anatomical nor representational, there is something organic and geometric about her works. The sensuality of the looping yarn suggests a certain softness, but the use of twine means this is only relative. The flexibility of the repeating stitches forms a fabric, a skin or a crust, depending on the nature of the yarn she is working with. Her art is fed by her own

emotions, but she allows others to react in their own way: 'My works are figurative and not realist. They are figures of fantasy. I turn indefinable things into reality.' Her sculptures are pliable; they can move a little or a lot, but they are never still. Sometimes they are not easy to manipulate but their flexibility gives them a kind of vitality.

Seaweed, coral and jellyfish shapes seem to form spontaneously in her work. Agnès now deliberately tries to distance herself from these, although the jellyfish remains a key motif for her. Encountered many times in her dreams, she sees it as representing a constant threat that she needs to deal with. People often compare her work to tribal art, suggesting that her creations have echoes of Oceanic and African art: 'I love what are called the "primitive" arts but I balk at the

Above:
The Head Snatcher
52 × 40 × 13 cm
Crocheted linen, 2013

suggestion of an obvious relationship. In fact I would hate to be an artist under the influence of others. I want to go beyond clichés and references.'

Some of her works are made using a single length of twine, rather like writing a text without lifting the pen from the paper. There are no cuts or additions: 'If you undid the last knot to unravel the twine, you would end up with one large ball of yarn made up of the original balls crocheted end to end.' Agnès compares the yarn she follows on her journey to the string Ariadne gave Theseus so that he could return to her after slaying the Minotaur: 'Each object crocheted with an unbroken length of twine is a labyrinth, and I am Theseus.'

PSEUDONYM
TRIXIE VON PURL

PLACE OF RESIDENCE
LEWES, UK

PLACE OF BIRTH
LONDON, UK

DATE OF BIRTH **1966**

WEBSITE
GERALDINEWARNER.COM

GERALDINE WARNER

Geraldine Warner, also known by the pseudonym Trixie von Purl, creates crocheted and knitted tableaux that tell stories. Like real-life cartoons, they retell the fairy tales of the Brothers Grimm, playfully illustrate the Kama Sutra or reinterpret the works of Jane Austen. Strongly influenced by pop culture and literature, the artist channels history, music and her own passion for textiles into her projects, without allowing any of them to dominate. Guided by the artists of the mid-20th century, Geraldine loves the textiles of Sonia Delaunay and Mary Whyte and the powerful images created by the photographer and painter László Moholy-Nagy. She is also inspired by the fashion and textiles of the first half of the 20th century, the true pioneers who

Opposite:
Supplies Closet
50 × 60 cm
Wool, cardboard, plywood, paper, wire, stuffing, beads
From the book *Knit Your Own Kama Sutra*, 2013

Above:
Vegas Baby
70 × 70 cm
Wool, cardboard, wood, paper, wire, stuffing, ribbons
From the book *Knit Your Own Kama Sutra*, 2013

explored the potential of knitting techniques, following in the footsteps of Elsa Schiaparelli, who cleverly introduced witty and unusual motifs and created knitwear influenced by graphic art. Geraldine also loves the work of Freddie Robins (see p. 228) and the playful and ambiguous sculptures of Cathie Pilkington. It was, however, the work of Lauren Child, the illustrator and author of children's books, which first gave her the idea of combining knitted objects and storytelling. Although many of her sources inspiration are not evident in the final product, she says they are always at the back of her mind when she is working.

Geraldine is one of a generation of craft addicts attracted by a recent revolution in the field of arts and crafts. Nonetheless, the arts have a complex relationship with the realm of crafts, and it saddens her that knitting and crochet are so often classified as hobbies rather than artforms.

Although she has practised a range of crafts and tried out many techniques, Geraldine has been knitting since childhood: when she was about seven years old, her mother and grandmother taught her the basics of this ever-present family pastime. Since then, she has been able to visualize, at a glance, what a completed work will look like: 'From that point on, my hands take over.' Drawn by the flexibility of knitting, she particularly likes its palette of colours and textures, and its ability to produce all kinds of shapes as well as happy accidents. When she wants to create a smooth knit texture for her small-scale subjects, she uses fine needles (2–3.5 mm) to avoid producing awkward gaps or holes. After deciding that she had spent too much time flirting with a variety of craft techniques without producing anything interesting, she chose to focus on knitting. Nevertheless

'I get a kick out of delving into my head, grabbing a bunch of sparking neurons which might not ever exist in the physical world and turning them into an actual object.'

she still uses painting, photography and digital graphics to create backdrops for her little woollen figures (supported by wire skeletons). She uses these to tell stories through photographs, and even sometimes through stop-motion animation.

Geraldine enjoys every step of the creative process, but especially planning the project and the research stage, which gives her the same sense of excitement she gets when starting anything new. When the making stage actually begins, she feels she has to keep going until the end, never giving up, even if problems crop up or if what she produces does not exactly match up what she'd originally imagined. But she always carries on, driven by the desire to create, always amazed by yarn's ability to become a 3D object, delighted that she is able to express herself in ways other than words.

Working in a spare room-turned-studio, overflowing with cupboards, baskets and drawers full of yarn, she creates highly detailed pieces, interpreting the world around her. Her works are never abstract and often include direct or indirect allusions: the farmyard scene in *Knit Your Own Kama Sutra*, for instance, features one of her figures wearing a dress inspired by Judy Garland in *The Wizard of Oz*. She claims to have no idea how Kansas found its way into a book about the Kama Sutra!

Right:
Emma & Harriet
80 × 100 cm
Wool, cardboard, plywood, paper, wire, stuffing, beads
From the book *Pride and Preju-Knits*, 2014

Opposite:
Colonel Brandon & Willoughby Fight a Duel
50 × 65 cm
Wool, cotton, cardboard, plywood, wire, stuffing, beads
From the book *Pride and Preju-Knits*, 2014

MARK NEWPORT

PLACE OF RESIDENCE
**KEEGO HARBOR,
MICHIGAN, USA**

PLACE OF BIRTH
**AMSTERDAM,
NEW YORK, USA**

DATE OF BIRTH **1964**

WEBSITE
**MARKNEWPORTARTIST.
COM**

Mark Newport is artist-in-residence and head of the Fiber Department at the Cranbrook Academy of Art in Michigan. He holds an MA in Fine Art from the School of the Art Institute of Chicago, where he studied fibre and design. He began to knit in the early 2000s and from then on gradually introduced knitting into his work. Surprised by the reaction of friends, family and passing strangers, who were amazed and sometimes appalled to see a man engaged in such a 'feminine' activity, Mark developed a print series called *Alter Egos* (above). They depict Mark himself knitting in a range of traditionally 'masculine' locations: on the stands at a football game (*At the Game*), backstage at a concert (*Backstage* and *Practice*), in military gear in a forest (*Commando*), on horseback like a cowboy (*Cowboy*) or in a bar (*Pick-Up*).

Inspired by pop culture and comic strips, the human body, vintage textiles and street art, as well as his own experiences, Mark does not claim to belong to any particular movement but cites Jane Lackey, Anne Wilson and Joan Livingstone as his mentors. His knits are made in acrylic yarn (because it is cheap and there is such a huge palette of colours) and mostly in stocking stitch, using US size 6 needles (4 mm). He specializes in knitting life-size superhero costumes, enjoying the slow pace of the process and its almost automatic associations with femininity, which clash with the stereotypical macho attributes of superheroes. Some of these costumes are interpretations of exisiting heroes from comics and films but most are imaginary figures like *Sweaterman*, *Argyleman* and *Bobbleman*. They all explore the contradictions that have grown up around the traditional American ideals of masculinity and heroism.

The Sweatermen are reinterpretations of conventional superhero costumes. For *Sweaterman 3* (p. 55), Mark's choice of colours and textures harked back to the sweaters knitted by his mother, who loved wool. The most recent costumes in the series are born from a mixture of his childhood experiences and his adult exploration of the need for protection and heroism. The costumes named *E*, *A*, *F* and *W Man* are knitted in colours taken from the natural world (sunsets, oceans, beaches, foliage), and represent the four elements of ancient philosophy: earth, air, fire and water. These four elements become each hero's superpowers while the cheap acrylic yarn contradicts the idea of the natural world: the hero's costume becomes a kind of armour or talisman that enables him to achieve great things, but it can also betray his body, revealing the vulnerability of flesh hidden beneath the thick knitted fabric.

Above:
At the Game and *Backstage*
from the series *Alter Egos*
each 33 × 48 cm
Inkjet prints, 2009

Left:
Argyleman
203 × 58.5 × 15 cm
Hand-knitted acrylic yarn
and buttons, 2007

Above:
Sweaterman 6
203 × 58.5 × 15 cm
Hand-knitted acrylic yarn
and buttons, 2010

Above left:
Ribbed
203 × 58.5 × 15 cm
Hand knitted acrylic yarn
and buttons, 2009

Above right:
Sweaterman 5
203 × 58.5 × 15 cm
Hand-knitted acrylic yarn
and buttons, 2008

Embodiments of the artist's childhood memories, images of the father that every little boy dreams of, of the man he once wanted to become when he grew up, these costumes signify masculinity and protection, but they are also images of vulnerability, paying tribute to Mark's mother who knitted acrylic jumpers for him, to protect him against the icy winters of New England. They are costumes that

the artist could put on to protect his family from bullies, murderers, terrorists, and messianic fanatics, or simply suits suspended from coat hangers that anyone could wear to become an instant superhero.

Mark also works with embroidery and is currently creating a series based around the concepts of mending and repairing, exploring the relationship between surgical stitches, textiles and scars.

Above left:
Sweaterman 3
203 × 58.5 × 15 cm
Hand-knitted acrylic yarn
and buttons, 2005

Above right:
Batman 3
203 × 58.5 × 15 cm
Hand-knitted acrylic yarn
and buttons, 2006

PLACE OF RESIDENCE
BRIGHTON, UK

PLACE OF BIRTH
SALLY: **LONDON, UK**
JOANNA: **ALNWICK,
NORTHUMBERLAND, UK**

DATE OF BIRTH
SALLY: **1954**
JOANNA: **1955**

WEBSITE
**MUIRANDOSBORNE.
CO.UK**

SALLY MUIR & JOANNA OSBORNE

Sally Muir and Joanna Osborne are knitwear designers linked by their love of dogs. Running their own knitwear shop, they also sell their clothes in many stores in the UK, the USA, Japan and Europe. Professional partners for more than thirty years, they put together two collections a year and several pieces of their knitted clothing are in the permanent collection of the Victoria and Albert Museum in London. They started by machine-knitting jumpers with animal motifs, famously including the 'black sheep' sweater worn by Princess Diana. Frustrated by the limitations of knitting machines, they began to knit by hand and showed their work in New York, Paris and Milan, and from then on concentrated on cashmere knitwear manufactured by a small team based in Nepal. Their knitted animals first appeared in 2010.

Joanna Osborne was taught to knit at the age of ten by her mother, and her first project was, ironically, a dog's coat with a horribly saggy neck. Sally Muir learned to knit at the same age, at school, taught by the formidable Sister Mary Joseph, and much later gained a degree in fine arts at Bath School of Art and Design. This degree opened the way to a new discipline for her: painting.

The duo love wool, preferably pure wool, which is so sumptuous that they feel they can excuse its price, using it because of its infinite potential, its warmth and cosiness, and its ability to make you feel cherished. They say that it has something magical about it and that with a ball of wool and two needles you can create almost anything.

Above:
Bulldog
15 × 11 cm, 2010

Opposite, above:
West Highland Terrier
15 × 12 cm, 2010

Opposite, below:
Afghan Hound
20 × 17 cm, 2010

From left to right:
German Shepherd, Old English Sheepdog, Border Collie, Rough Collie, Corgi, Husky, 2010

Preferring knitting to crochet, despite its slower pace, because of the results it can achieve and its more gratifying possibilities, the pair generally work with 2¾ mm needles, creating dogs, cats and all kinds of animals in detail. The challenge is finding the right basic shape while staying true to the breed and ensuring a perfect join between the muzzle and the head, which can be very tricky. The artists use pipe cleaners to give their little animals stability, and strengthen their life-size models with a framework of aluminium wire. The finishing-off stage is the most satisfying part of the process. When they are first stuffed, the dogs look a little unformed. But once they've been given ears, eyes and a tail, the

'*We have always owned dogs; they have been an integral part of our lives.*'

dogs look stunningly lifelike. With eight books now completed, Sally and Joanna seem to want to reproduce the entire animal kingdom in wool, working closer to the world of crafts than contemporary art. They are happy to knit any breed of dog or cat, as well as penguins, crocodiles and even dinosaurs, building up a woolly Noah's Ark that is guaranteed to raise a smile.

Opposite:
Bengal Cat
25 × 11 cm, 2011

Above:
Black and White Cat
18 × 13 cm, 2011

Right:
Poodle
17 × 18 cm, 2010

CAMILLE DUPUIS

PSEUDONYM **CAM DUP**

PLACE OF RESIDENCE
CHOISY-LE-ROI, FRANCE

PLACE OF BIRTH
SURESNES, FRANCE

DATE OF BIRTH **1984**

WEBSITE
CAMDUP.COM

Camille Dupuis's work, her passion for textile design and her personal life are all connected. She works as a freelancer, often with friends, and was a member of the Ateliers d'Art de France, the major organization for people working in the arts: 'I felt part of the family when I was with them.' A graduate in applied arts, she does not see herself as belonging to any particular movement, and simply says she is 'one of those people who love materials'. She is intensely curious and interested in alternative lifestyles, such as zero waste, minimalism

and veganism. Her imagination is fired by books on science, mythology and religious art, but she also draws inspiration from the materials themselves: 'If I like it or feel it has been neglected, I ask myself what I can make from it.' Following this reasoning, Camille might, for example, cover pots of paint with knitting or create pieces out of old pairs of tights.

Meeting Aurélie Mathigot (see p. 212), with whom she apprenticed after her studies, proved a turning point in her career: 'Aurélie is one of those people who have genuinely reinvented the rules of yarn,

Above and opposite:
Knitted Paint Pots
Max. height 20 cm
Empty paint pots, machine knitting, recycled yarn,
2010–14

Above:
Fossil Telephone
Height 22 cm
Telephone, felted wool
and sweater, 2010

by crocheting objects, using metallic or fluorescent yarn or even rope, and exhibiting her work in art galleries.' Camille loves the poetic and precise work of Anu Tuominen, which ranges from textiles to paper and land art, and yet is always totally straightforward. She also admires Odilon Redon for his 'hallucinatory' colours and mysticism, and Jean Lurçat for his personality and his bold tapestries.

In 2007, at the Françoise Conte School of Art in Paris, she learned to use a knitting machine and then to felt her knitted work. From the outset Camille was drawn to this technique, asking for the key to the classroom so that she could go on knitting after lessons ended, until the day when she rediscovered her grandmother's knitting machine: 'I also knit a great deal by hand: it offers more possibilities.' Although hand knitting is a nomadic, quiet, zen-like activity, she does find it somewhat slow, which is why she prefers to use a knitting machine for some pieces; although it is more restrictive, it can produce a great variety of motifs and rapid results. In 2016, an eight-month trip around Latin America also opened her mind to new ideas.

One day a teacher showed her knitted works made of pure new wool that had been felted in a washing machine. The blurred motifs and dense fabric seemed magical to her. The same evening, Camille decided to experiment at home, and from then on, felting and fulling became her favourite new techniques.

She enjoys working with wool because of its unique properties: it is warm, stretchy and elastic; it can be felted and, once dyed, its colours stay very bright. However, Camille no longer knits with animal fibres, much as she loves their natural, ecological and renewable aspects, since learning that sheep do not voluntarily give up their wool and that the production of wool is the result of the human oppression of animals: 'In large-scale farming, they are regarded as merchandise and can be seriously mistreated, using cruel techniques such as "mulesing" (surgically removing skin from around the sheep's bottom to prevent disease). Even in smallholdings that treat their animals with more respect, the animals end up in the slaughterhouse.' When she became a vegan, Camille decided to stop supporting this violent industry and now she actively tries to work with vegetable fibres.

'I like it when these materials are re-embroidered; it makes them look brighter and richer.'

Silent Boom Boom Box
50 × 34 cm
Recycled foam and
machine knitting,
recycled yarn, 2011

Above and left:
Taxidermy
Each *c.* 36 × 36 cm
Hand-knitted wool,
fabric, 2010–14

Knitting with 5–15 mm needles, she mainly uses reclaimed yarn, which offers an extremely varied palette as well as a way of giving new value to discarded scraps of material: 'Apart from that, I also love the kitschest fibre of all: lurex!' She is most inspired during the early stages of her work, when she is carried away by her imagination: 'I go rushing off in every direction, like at the beginning of a love affair.'

Camille knits in order to communicate, to express herself, and to try and capture what cannot be said in words: 'That is also why I love making animals, in an attempt to understand what links us to them.' There is of course also the simple pleasure of creating, of transforming the material. It is an act she finds gratifying and likes to share: 'When you work with needles, time stops. It is an activity that is both meditative and time-consuming.'

Her body of work, highly figurative and inspired by animals, plants and everyday objects, is now growing more colourful and geometric. It is often said that her pieces are poetic and full of wit, and she takes that as a compliment: 'It's a special moment when a client or friend is moved by one of my creations.'

TRACY WIDDESS

PLACE OF RESIDENCE
**VANCOUVER ISLAND,
CANADA**

PLACE OF BIRTH
**VANCOUVER ISLAND,
CANADA**

DATE OF BIRTH **1976**

WEBSITE
**BRUTAL-KNITTING.
TUMBLR.COM**

Tracy Widdess describes herself as a hyperactive artist; her fingers never stop moving. Knitting is the only thing she truly loves doing and creating is her only means of feeling good, physically and emotionally, even though she often feels like one lifetime will never be enough to achieve everything she want to do and finish all the projects that are germinating inside her head.

In 2000, Tracy's flatmate first taught her how to knit and crochet. She was attracted from the start by the dexterity required and the technique's lack of popularity and soon decided to experiment with knitting and

Above:
Mayan Headdress
50 × 50 cm, 2015

Opposite:
Regent
70 × 45 cm, 2014

Above left:
Krampus
40 × 50 cm, 2012

Above right:
Skull
45 × 30 cm, 2013

Below left:
Insect
60 × 35 cm, 2013

Below right:
Predator
30 × 40 cm, 2011

specialize in it. Rather than following traditional, formal instructions, she taught herself, hunting for motifs without using preliminary sketches or designs, until she had fully mastered her tools: 'It took me ages to reach this level of competence.' Tracy's work is inspired contemporary artists like Jake and Dinos Chapman, famed for their chaotic scenes marked by inertia, indifference and detachment, and also by the work of Théo Mercier, a young sculptor and set designer, and his explorations of anthropology, ethnography, geopolitics and tourism, and by the American artist Paul McCarthy, famous for his inflatable sculptures, especially his controversial *Tree*, displayed in the

Opposite:
Head
85 × 65 cm, 2015
In collaboration with
Stéphane Blanquet

Place Vendôme in Paris in October 2014. Influenced by all of these, Tracy Widdess creates scary monsters, knitted in wool, inspired by the world of sci-fi and comic books. Describing her work as 'brutal knitting', she fuses hand knitting and machine knitting to produce phantasmagorical masks and hoods that are both surprising and witty. She allows herself a month to complete each of her works, which is as much time as she thinks she needs to stay sane, and gives them evocative names: *Jabberwocky*, the monster from Lewis Carroll's *Through the Looking-Glass*; *Krampus* (p. 70) inspired by the mythical, anthropomorphic creature, covered in hair and with two large horns on its head, who according to east European folklore accompanies the Christmas visits of St Nicholas; or *Venom*, a symbiotic alien from Marvel Comics.

Above:
Boobs
120 × 70 cm, 2015
In collaboration with
Stéphane Blanquet

Right:
Hindrance
28 × 35 cm, 2014

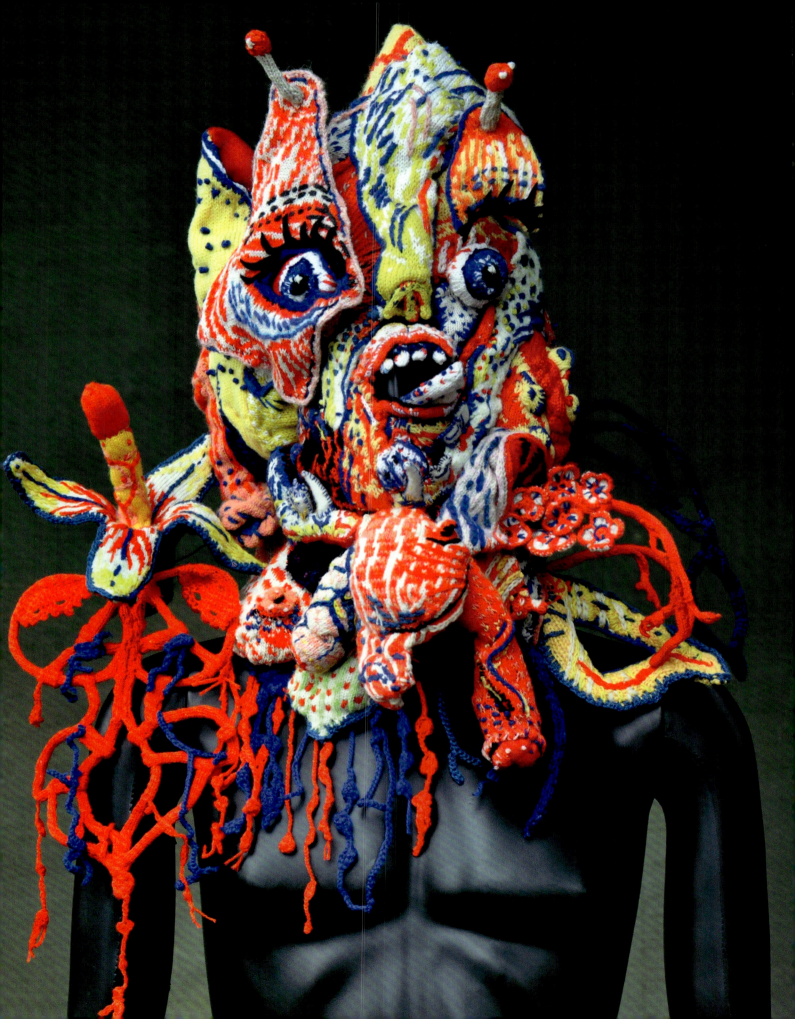

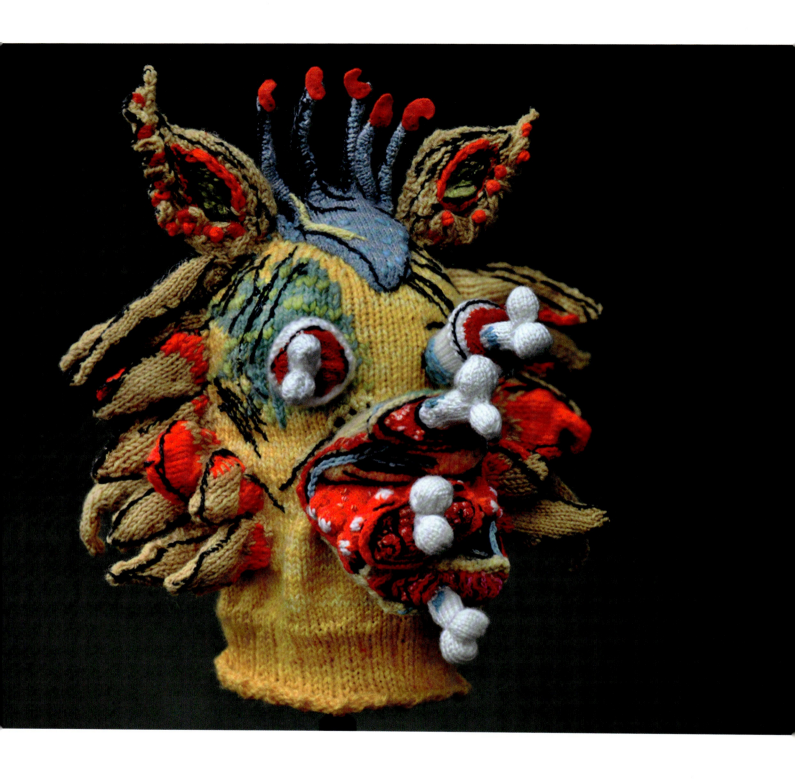

Above:
Dog Mask
35 × 40 cm, 2014

Tracy also collaborates with other artists and translates their works into three dimensions. These include the graphic artist and designer Stéphane Blanquet, with whom she created *Boobs* (p. 72) and *Head* (p. 73), and the illustrator Dieter Van der Ougstraete, for whom she has created friendly monsters. Extremely focused on detail and precision, combining the techniques of knitting, crocheting and embroidery, her chimerical figures and masks evoke childhood fears and recall old-fashioned and often disquieting ethnological illustrations of unknown tribal societies.

Using 3 mm (or sometimes finer) needles and very fine yarn specially designed for machine knitting – yarn that she can double or triple to achieve the right thickness – in bold and sometimes clashing colours from a palette that can verge on kitsch, Tracy Widdess pushes the limits of knitting, drawing on her exuberant imagination, and giving free rein to her whims.

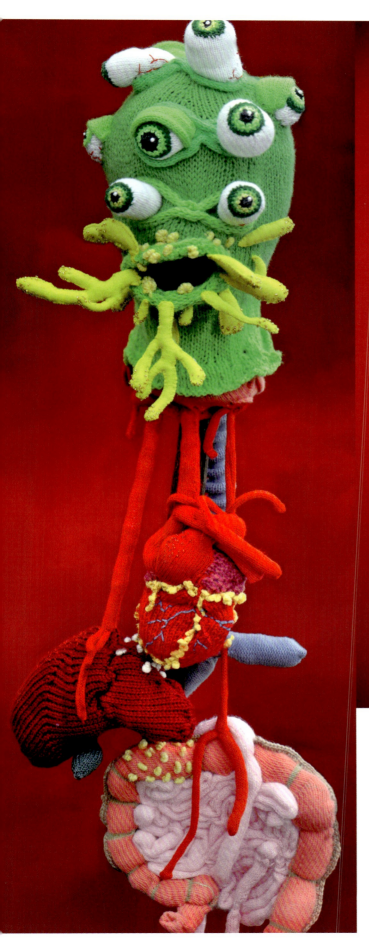

Left:
Penanggallan
100 × 45 cm, 2012

Above:
*Why Be Yourself
When You Can Be A
Decorative Ulcer*
50 × 40 cm, 2013

DAINA TAIMINA

PLACE OF RESIDENCE
ITHACA, NEW YORK, USA

PLACE OF BIRTH
RIGA, LATVIA

DATE OF BIRTH **1954**

Daina Taimina is famed for her crochet work, but is also a mathematician and Adjunct Associate Professor at Cornell University. All of her sculptures are derived from the same basic concept – the hyperbolic plane, a surface in which space constantly curves away from itself – and illustrate all the varieties of two-dimensional hyperbolic planes. She says that once completed, each piece sometimes takes on its best form naturally, while others have to be coaxed into the right shapes. That is when something unexpected can emerge.

In 1997 she began to crochet models of hyperbolic planes and used them as teaching tools in her non-Euclidean geometry course. Her models then became popular among geometry teachers in universities and schools and in 2005 she was invited to take part in the exhibition *Not The Knitting You Know*, at which she presented *Hyperbolic Mystery*, one of her first yarn sculptures. She then began to research ways of giving her teaching tools a more artistic quality, swapping the cheap acrylic yarn she used for her courses for good-quality woollen yarn.

Above and opposite:
Two models from the
Manifold I series
30 × 30 × 45 cm
Cotton, 2009

Day and Night in Hyperbolic Space, created in 2007, is an extension of her experiments with different kinds of yarn. Aiming to combine two colours, after finding that a single skein of yarn was not enough to complete the whole object, Daina Taimina expected the two shades to mix chaotically throughout the work, but they did not. The work's title was inspired by one side of the piece being predominantly dark blue, and the other being predominantly pale.

At the *Mathcounts* exhibition at the University of Connecticut in 2006, she took part in a round table with the French artist Bernar Venet, famous for his steel sculptures, and went on talking to him afterwards. He told her he liked her works but that she should make them on a larger scale. This idea gave birth to *Hyperbolic Space*, or, more precisely, *Global Warm(r)ing*. Originally, this pink crochet work, which symbolizes the urgent issue of climate change, was to be shown standing on a large macramé work representing the earth

'I was surprised how differently the same shape came to life.'

consumed by global warming. At first, Daina only had 88 skeins of pink yarn to work with, but she then found another 38 on eBay, which enabled her to enlarge the piece to its present size and consequently have the work included in *Guinness World Records* in 2013 as the largest ever crocheted hyperbolic surface.

The piece entitled *Fuzzy*, created in 2011, is made of mixed fibres. It is based on a mathematical idea and is tempting to touch. Daina

thinks that perhaps it should have been entitled *Remedy for Anxiety About Maths.*

The *Manifold II* series (opposite) serves as a tribute to William Thurston, renowned for his work on three-dimensional geometry and topology but also for having changed the way an entire generation perceives mathematics. One day Thurston gave her a small paper model and asked if she could reproduce it in crochet. She took up the challenge and completed the work in August 2012. Unfortunately, the mathematician died before she had the chance to show it to him. Over the two days after his death, she created another piece and continued experimenting, always bearing in mind what he had written in the foreword to her book *Crocheting Adventures with Hyperbolic Planes*: 'Mathematics sings when we feel it in our whole brain. People are generally inhibited about even trying to share their personal mental models. People like music, but they are afraid to sing. You only learn to sing by singing.'

JÜRG BENNINGER

PLACE OF RESIDENCE
**BIEL/BIENNE,
SWITZERLAND**

PLACE OF BIRTH
**ALTDORF,
SWITZERLAND**

DATE OF BIRTH **1966**

WEBSITE **JJWB.CH**

Winner of a Swiss
Art Award, 2006

Jürg Benninger refuses to make judgments about what is good or bad. He loves monsters, comedy 'and anything that opens up the heart and mind.' Not a member of any movement, choosing to take his own senses as his only guides, he draws his inspiration from everyday life, trying to live and work with his heart and his mind, and always believing that he must not view himself as the centre of the universe.

After a foundation year at Lucerne Art School, he moved towards graphic art, seeing textiles as part of a more feminine world than he felt he could embrace as a young man. He briefly worked in advertising, trying to make a living in a job that left

Above:
Les Bêtes Heureuses
70 × 35 cm
Wool, foam, wire, 2011

Opposite:
Landing of the Amazons
200 × 125 cm
Wool, 2001

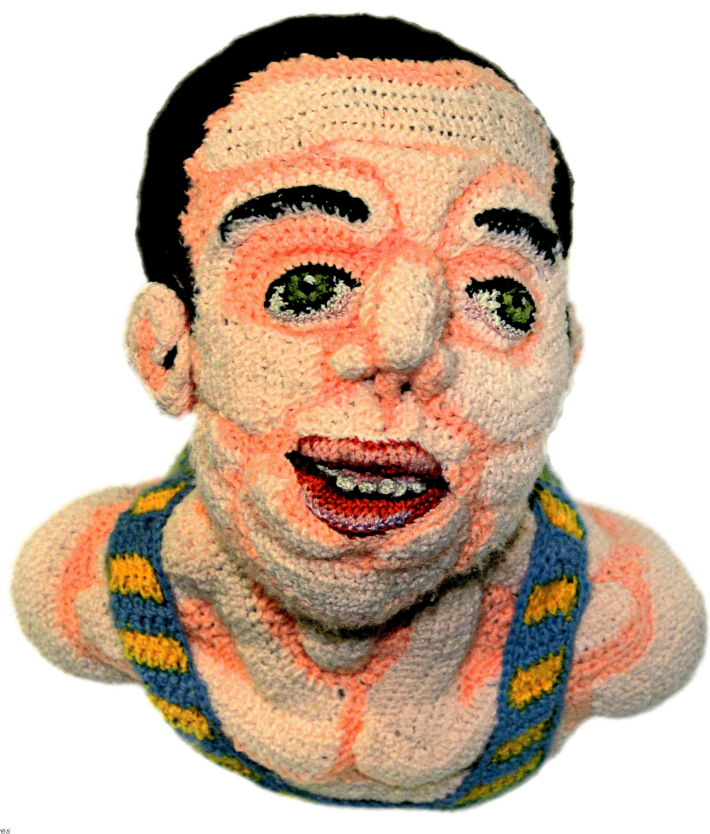

Yves
33 × 38 × 35 cm
Wool, foam, 2011

Man with Bird
34 × 47 cm
Wool, wire, foam, 2011

him enough time to devote himself to his own art. He then turned to painting for a few years, moving on to painted wood. In 2000, while he was staying at the Cité International des Arts in Paris, Jürg searched for a technique that would enable him to create large-format works without the constraints imposed by large, solid canvases. This is when he first discovered crochet and also wool, a material that was practical, soft and warm. From this point on, he was able to work without the limits of a format.

Crochet allows him to work slowly, letting his art evolve and develop in either two or three dimensions. Jürg crochets, packs up his work, stuffs it into a bag, moves around, and carries on elsewhere, while the work continues to grow. This technique frees him from constraints and allows him to work spontaneously, while also producing sophisticated works, full of imagination, wit and frivolity and, on closer attention, a certain ambiguity. What seems light-hearted at first sight (the shapes, the woollen texture and the colours that seem to ask to be touched) can then prove oddly disconcerting. Jürg often

'The general public often regards the technique of crochet, mainly practised by women, as an activity that's both trivial and recreational.'

Opposite:
Prince no. 5
192 × 256 × 55 cm
Wool, 2002

Below:
We'll Laugh You To Death
130 × 40 × 80 cm
Wool, wire, foam, 2013

uses his own experiences and intimate feelings as subjects for his artworks. When he begins a piece, generally using wool, he never knows how it will end up. Each of his creations requires a particular technique and specific materials and in most cases, a moment will come when he begins to doubt the whole thing and is prepared to give it up entirely and throw it away: 'But I love the before and the after.'

Left:
Exhibition at the ART-ETAGE gallery, Biel, Switzerland, 2016

AGATA
OLEK

PLACE OF RESIDENCE
NEW YORK, USA

PLACE OF BIRTH
STASZÓW, POLAND

DATE OF BIRTH **1978**

WEBSITE
OLEKNYC.COM

Agata Olek, better known simply as Olek, grew up in socialist Poland, at a time when, as she says, everybody was Catholic, white, and spoke only Polish. A stranger in her own land, she felt her beliefs, way of dressing and philosophy clashed with the post-Communist era of workers' agitation, a time when Lech Walesa was founding Solidarity and she was still calling herself Agata Oleksiak. Even if she did not like it at the time, she says, growing up in a socialist country made her what she is. As a child, she learned how to make art out of nothing, transforming anything that came into her house, anything she could keep, such as the coloured metal tops of the milk bottles that were delivered every morning and that she turned into Christmas decorations.

Olek graduated in cultural studies from Adam Mickiewicz University in Poznań, Poland. The title of her thesis was 'The symbolism of costumes in the films of Peter Greenaway'. During her research, she met Polish costume designer Barbara Ptak, who gave her many pieces of advice, one of which stayed in her mind afterwards: if you

Above left:
Happiness is an Inside Job
Crochet, various
yarns, 2013

Above:
Crocheted Scuba Diver
In collaboration with PangeaSeed, Mexico
Crochet, various yarns, 2015

want to design costumes, don't stay in Poland. Go to New York, and above all, don't say you're a beginner. Just act confident. Six days later, she moved to New York, where she enrolled in a sculpture course at LaGuardia Community College and began a career as a costume maker, which then led her towards sculpture and installation art.

She first learned to crochet at primary school, at an after-school class. When she came home, she grabbed a crochet hook and carried on until she had mastered its use, before eventually giving it up. In bed one day at the age of sixteen, she rediscovered her crocheting talents and began to make little hats, then backpacks for her friends, which she swapped for books. Then her love affair with crochet paused yet again. Later, however, after moving to New York, she used crochet for some of her costume work and realized, as she was putting a piece together, that it was crochet that had chosen her. At the time, her sculpture teacher at LaGuardia Community College was encouraging her to make works from unusual materials, such as rope, string or even fabric, and urged her to find a means of combining

Above:
Elephant Ball
Lancaster House, London
Crochet, various yarns,
2013

Opposite:
*Wars Come And Go And
The Carousel Is Always
There To Remind Us Of
The Good Times*
'Magic City' exhibition,
Dresden, Germany
Crochet, various
yarns, 2016

them. After spending the night trying to work out the best way to join the pieces together, she ended up trying crochet. She says it worked and that since then she has been crocheting. Using different sizes of crochet hook, and sometimes her fingers or arms for certain types of work, she will crochet anything from extremely fine lace to large inflatable objects, but she rarely uses wool or natural fibres since her pieces are meant to be shown outdoors. In a relationship that veers between love and hate, she spends hour upon hour creating, mingling her art and her life. Olek crochets stitch by stitch, minute after minute, often expecting to give up. Yet she feels that crochet has such incredible power and produces such surprising results that she sticks with it, even though the technique is slow and time-consuming and at times discouraging. She believes she makes

'I want to bring colour, life, energy and surprise to the living space.'

the best decisions when she is running out of time. The scale on which she works, which can be challenging and sometimes stressful, can force her to question the time or materials she will need. But when the moment of installation arrives, when everything begins to make sense, she finally feels the excitement and sense of satisfaction that the creative process brings.

Olek draws her inspiration from life, basing her work on real feelings, experiences and ideas. Inspired in particular by people she meets, and especially by the issues of human rights and oppression in the world, she says that for her, life, crochet and art are inseparable.

In her short film entitled *In the Blink of an Eye*, the camera slowly pans through the various rooms of a house of which every item, each piece of furniture, is crocheted. The crochet, which is bright and bold, reveals the beauty of things. And then, suddenly, the peace of the house is destroyed by several explosions that reduce it to rubble, obliterating the crocheted phrase 'All We Need is Love & Money'

and showing the speed at which everything we have built can be lost. According to her research, in 2015, over 27.8 million people in 127 countries lost their homes as a result of violence, conflict or disasters.

Olek believes that her work is never finished and that the continuing reactions of the public help to keep it alive. Its existence serves merely as a tool to help people become aware of their own emotions,

Crocheted Homeless Shelter, Delhi, India
Crochet, various yarns, 2015

to question, to reflect, to act and to enjoy. She says that she wants to create colour, life, energy and surprise. Taking as her role models Louise Bourgeois and the Serbian performance artist Marina Abramović, to name but two, Olek says she belongs to a movement that could be likened to that of freedom of expression, producing crochet work not only in her New York studio but also in Poland, Germany, Russia, France, Spain, India, Sweden, Finland, Brazil, Chile, Canada, Mexico, China, Taiwan, Hong Kong and around the world.

Above:
Train That Stood Still
Lodz, Poland
Crochet, various yarns, 2014

Below:
Olek and her Crocheted Army
Installation by Mark Dean Veca,
Virginia MOCA, Virginia Beach, VA
Crochet, various yarns, 2016

Right:
Saint Agatha, La Torera
Delimbo Gallery,
Seville, Spain
Crochet, various yarns, 2013

Her installations and performances are based around the social reality of diverse communities. In a spirit of interconnection, she wants to present her creations to an ever larger public and, as a militant supporter of women's rights, to bear witness to the equality of the sexes and freedom of expression, using her work to express her solidarity with all the oppressed of the world. *Working Woman in White: A Portrait* perfectly encapsulates her philosophy. In this performance, given at the BWA Gallery in Sanok, Poland, in March 2009, Olek's body became a ready-made. Inside an immaculate room, its ceiling covered with crocheted wool, the artist sat naked, perched on a chair more than two metres high, crocheting a kind of white blanket, a suit of armour or chrysalis that slowly covered her body, the loose stitches constantly multiplying. Then she pulled on a piece of yarn and undid every stitch. Once the armour had dissolved, Agata Olek crocheted it onto her body again, and so on: she knows she can continue this process forever, even when she feels she is running out of strength. The work loses its material presence in the midst of the process of creation, yet its destruction allows it to take physical form once again. She believes that everything is interchangeable, be it immobile or in metamorphosis, ancient or new, unique or ephemeral, public or private, hidden or exposed, performer or creator, traditional or innovative, unravelling or being reborn.

Above:
*Getting a Leg Over:
Hyperactive*
Height 16 cm
Marionette parts,
cotton, wadding, 2013

CÉCILE DACHARY

PLACE OF RESIDENCE
**BOULLAY-LES-TROUX,
FRANCE**

PLACE OF BIRTH
POITIERS, FRANCE

DATE OF BIRTH **1963**

WEBSITE
CECILEDACHARY.COM

Member of the Ateliers d'Art
de France and of the collective
Fiber Art Fever!

Following a childhood in provincial France, a course at a college of applied arts, a career as textile designer and collections assistant for children's fashion brands like Cacharel and Jacadi, since 2001 Cécile Dachary has devoted herself entirely to her art. In 2013 she decided that fabric and yarn were the obvious way to move forward: 'I came across a ball of white cotton and a crochet hook that I must have kept after a stay with my grandmother, who taught me to crochet when I was a little girl.'

Her grandmothers taught her to crochet, embroider and knit; her mother taught her basic sewing. Having inherited this family skill, she retains the memory of these symbolic crafts, once restricted to the intimacy of the home, and tries to broaden their scope. She now views the distinctly feminine, submissive and dated associations of yarnwork as a means of emancipation and personal expression. The slow pace of the process, its intensive nature and the patience required, together with its relative cheapness, distance it from contemporary issues of consumerism and the dictates of speed and profit.

Cécile works mainly with cotton rather than wool: its colour and thickness are the determining factors. Because it is so fine, she finds that cotton allows her to emphasize volume. The stitches are small, almost invisible to the naked eye, and the technique seems to

Left:
Getting a Leg Over: Alone
Height 16 cm
Marionette parts,
cotton, wadding, 2013

Below:
Breast Udders
Height 80 cm
Cotton, wadding, 2009

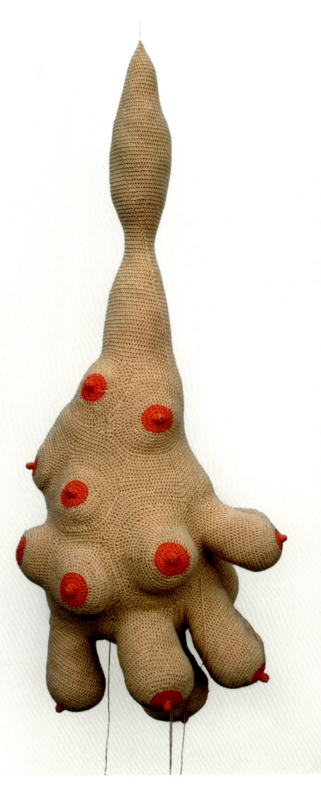

Left:
Getting a Leg Over: Caterpillar
Height 23 cm
Marionette parts, cotton, wadding, 2013

Above:
Skin
20 × 25 cm
Cotton, 2008

Above and left:
Big Skin
200 × 250 cm
Butcher's twine, 2011

disappear. The thickness of wool, by constrast, gives those projects a greater sense of presence and vivacity.

Crochet, usually with a 1.5 mm hook, gives Cécile freedom because it is so simple and flexible. It is easy to create volume and to change colours. In addition, there is no need to count the stitches, unlike in knitting. Improvisation seems to happen by itself. Drawing on a variety of influences, such as life, the body, love, sex and different materials, Cécile crochets in an almost trance-like state, following the regular rhythm of the stitches. She works the textile till it becomes like a second skin, an envelope for the body, breathing life into it and giving it fleshly reality. As a form of physical protection, it reflects memories, entire or splintered, multiple or moving, troubling or violent, sensual or erotic. The yarn becomes a motif that echoes the artist's emotions, as her intuition takes her from detailed figurative expression to the crudest and most primitive of

Above and opposite:
Wall Trophies
Height 35–90 cm
Cotton, wool, acrylic
yarn, 2015

shapes: full circle. She creates organic volumes that become idiosyncratic representations of the human body, its surface and its substance, the organs with their microscopic cells, and even bacteria, which she turns into fantastical dream-like images, revealing the intimate secrets within. This fascination with organs and skin dates from the days when, as a child, she used to watch her grandmother kill, skin and gut rabbits: 'There was nothing repellent about it because she worked so cleanly. I was bewitched by those magnificent remains.'

Although the human body remains at the centre of her work, memory and time are also guiding themes. Moving away from the body as a subject, Cécile began to work with the themes of trophies (pp. 100–1) and the city (opposite), for which she tried to create the feel of old sheets, marked by the traces of life, the memory of bodies and the passage of time. Producing a large-format work puts her patience and willpower to the test, as in the work entitled *Big Skin* (p. 99), which took more than ten months to complete. She never gives up, never lets doubt take over, keeps crocheting stitches one by one, often putting a work aside and then returning to it a few days later. Tolerating the strain of the yarn on her fingers and the weight of the entire work, she crochets until she is ready to give up, and then feels a great satisfaction in seeing the completed piece.

Alongside her textile work, Cécile experiments with other materials, including ceramics, which she is now trying to combine with yarn and crochet.

'I hope these techniques will continue to be used forever, as a tribute to women here and elsewhere and to earlier generations.'

Above and opposite:
The City
Variable dimensions
White cotton, pebbles, 2012

FELIEKE
VAN DER LEEST

PLACE OF RESIDENCE
ØYSTESE, NORWAY

PLACE OF BIRTH
EMMEN, NETHERLANDS

DATE OF BIRTH **1968**

WEBSITE
**FELIEKEVANDERLEEST.
COM**

Felieke van der Leest is a jeweler and artist who creates portable sculptures from textiles, precious metals and plastic toys. Trained at the MTS Vakschool in Schoonhoven and the Gerrit Rietveld Academie in Amsterdam, she is a qualified goldsmith, silversmith and jeweler.

The head of jewelry at the Rietveld Academie, Ruudt Peters, became her mentor. She says he always knew she would find her path but that she struggled a lot to discover it. She is also very grateful to her high-school biology teacher, the first person who mentioned the idea of applying to a technical college for goldsmithing – after noticing some earrings Felieke had made herself – and to the art jeweler Sylvia Blickman, a teacher at the Rietveld Academie, who suggested she take courses in jewelry. Felieke had been doing courses in drawing and painting but did not enjoy them. She subsequently discovered that what she really loves is small-scale, three-dimensional work.

Inspired by everything around her, she likes to absorb information slowly before using it, keeping it at the back of her mind for a while

Above left:
Mr Zen
14 × 6 × 6 cm
Polyester/polyamide and viscose, plastic animal, mother-of-pearl, glass, silver, alpaca, 2015

Opposite, above right:
Prairie Pioneer
15 × 10 × 10 cm
Cotton, polyester/polyamide, viscose, lightweight
felt, plastic animal, glass beads, glass, silver, leather,
14-carat gold, 2012
Textiel Museum, Tilburg, and KODE Art Museums, Bergen

Below:
Billy Bang
12 × 8 × 3 cm
Polyester/polyamide, lightweight felt, plastic
animal, 14-carat gold, silver, Swarovski crystal,
sapphires, 2009
National Museum of Scotland, Edinburgh

Above:
Peek-a Puma
7 × 5 × 1.5 cm, 2014

Opposite:
*Jewelrassic:
An Inside Story*
15 × 11 × 6 cm
Polyester/polyamide,
plastic animal, oxidized
silver, aluminium, paper,
plastic, zirconium, 2017
CODA Museum,
Apeldoorn, Netherlands

and then letting it emerge by itself. But her strongest influence is probably her childhood. Her parents ran a company dealing in cranes, bulldozers and trucks used for transporting sand, and sometimes had to move large animals such as circus elephants and rhinoceroses. Yet this childhood spent in contact with animals does not fully explain why she loves to transform them in her work. She draws her inspiration from popular culture and folktales involving cats, foxes and other animals wearing clothes and shoes, speaking our language and behaving like humans.

The animals that lie at the heart of her work, whether as jewelry, objects or lamps, lead full social lives and play the leading role in fantastical fairytales. But the stories Felieke tells can be read at different levels and the artist likes to allow viewers to find their own interpretations. In fact, she prefers questions to statements, even though, at first sight, her works seem figurative and easy to read. And although it is hard not to smile at her art, she does not

Right:
Lunatitia Velociraptorina
14 × 7 × 7 cm
Polyester/polyamide, viscose,
plastic animal, argentite,
zirconium, alpaca, 2016

*'When I work with colours
I feel I am painting.
When I work with metal
I feel I am constructing.
When I work with toys
I feel like a child.'*

see humour as a point of departure but simply as the end result of a process. Using both irony and satire, she makes playful use of the comic effects of illogicality. The lack of logic can sometimes camouflages serious ideas, and is what prevents us from taking conceited people seriously. She particularly targets sportsmen and macho stereotypes, criticizing their false values and superficial lifestyles. In the bracelet called *The J. Russells* (opposite), a row of dog-headed soccer players form a defensive wall, their paws over their genitals,

while their striped outfits recall not only football shirts but also the costumes of cartoon convicts.

Powered by the joy and wonder of making, and by the idea of turning her thoughts into reality, she crochets with Madeira brand thread, which is very fine and colourful, combining it with metallic yarn, plastic toys, gold, silver and gemstones.

Right:
Snow White
11 × 5 × 3 cm
Polyester/polyamide, viscose, plastic
animal, 14-carat white gold, 2007

Above:
Sharky Boy
10 × 10 × 4.5 cm
Polyester/polyamide, viscose,
plastic animal, 14-carat white gold,
galvanized glass beads, topaz, 2009

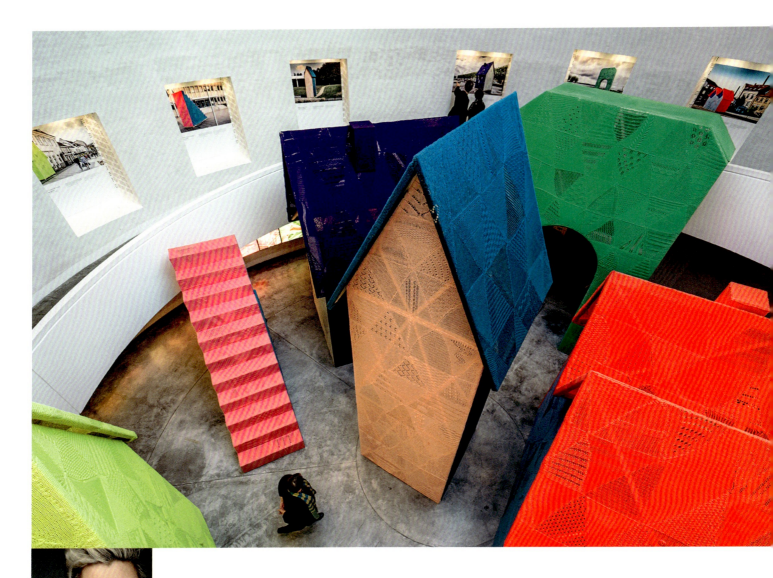

ISABEL BERGLUND

PLACE OF RESIDENCE
**COPENHAGEN,
DENMARK**

PLACE OF BIRTH
**COPENHAGEN,
DENMARK**

DATE OF BIRTH **1972**

WEBSITE
ISABELBERGLUND.DK

Isabel Berglund's works are concerned with notions of identity and surface; they can be simultaneously figurative and abstract, rigid and flexible, suggesting presence and absence, the expected and the unexpected.

After graduating from the Danish School of Design in Copenhagen, she moved to London where, as an Erasmus student, she studied textiles at Chelsea College of Art and Design, before doing a master's in fashion knitwear at Central Saint Martins. During her training she became fascinated by knitting, a technique that allowed her to create large surfaces as well as three-dimensional volumes. She taught herself to use a knitting machine then later learned to knit by hand.

Pushing at the limits of the old-fashioned image evoked by knitting, she started integrating it into an artistic context. The close relationship between the title of each work and the process of creating it has a strong impact on the final result; she is keen to create a dialogue between the story of a concrete object and the idea she is trying to evoke through her work. Taking inspiration

Above:
*Monument of Stitches –
A Social Art Project*
550 × 1000 × 1000 cm
Knitting, mixed acrylic/
wool yarn, wood, 2016

Opposite:
*Floating Island of Pearls –
A Social Art Project*
670 × 600 × 350 cm
Knitting, wood, acrylic
paint, mixed acrylic/
wool yarn, 2014

'I wondered how to describe the
relationship between body and space.'

from everyday life, she likes to work with ordinary objects, objects
with their own imagery or symbolism, or that say something about
our history or our way of life. These objects often reflect puns and
other linguistic concepts, allowing them to be interpreted in poetic
and emotional terms. Evoking a sense of childhood, the works can
become a space for experimentation, a place where the borders of the
human and material worlds merge.

Isabel is inspired by artists as diverse as Meret Oppenheim, Man
Ray, Mike Kelley, Louise Bourgeois, Sarah Lucas and Jessica Stock-
holder. A common theme runs through her works, in which she
allows other materials to play a part but always uses knitting as her
main technique. She also creates works in wood, which she transforms into knitted pieces. Using a variety of different needle sizes and
yarn of all kinds, which she chooses to suit her current project, she
works at a variety of scales and creates installations that become, in a
sense, spaces within a space. She plays with the public's perception of
her work: the way people may be disturbed by the realistic aspect of
the pieces but also by the contrasts between the textures used. Some
sculptures contain elements that invite viewers to cocoon themselves
within and feel the work from the inside. In this way, her installations
are both garments and habitats.

City of Stitches (right), a work it took fourteen people and several
months to complete, merges design, art and fashion and questions
the concept of boundaries between the arts. This conceptual installation invites the public to become part of the finished work by
putting on the clothes that hang from its knitted walls. As a result, the
visitors, now clothed in white, disappear into the walls and become
one with the piece. A tree, placed at the centre, asks the question: is
it inside or outside the work, which, like snow, envelops the body
and muffles the sound of voices? The clear ambiguity of the relationship between outside and inside, as well as the witty invitation to a
moment of contemplation, turn this imposingly proportioned work
into an aesthetic and interactive experience.

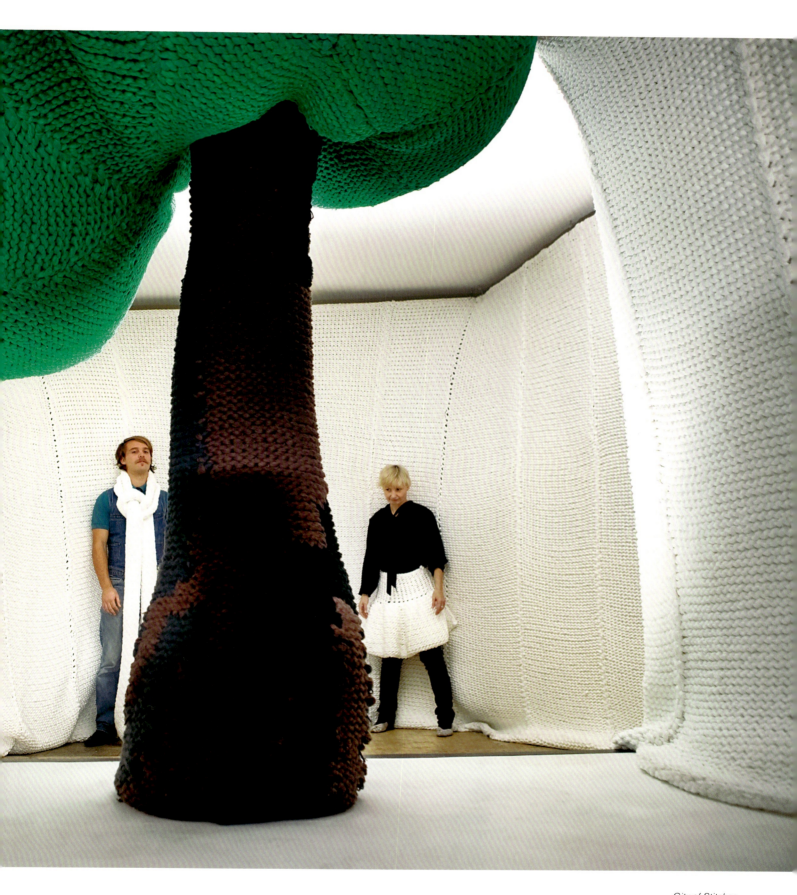

City of Stitches
350 × 250 × 280 cm
Knitting, cotton yarn,
wood, 2004

JOANA VASCONCELOS

PLACE OF RESIDENCE
LISBON, PORTUGAL

PLACE OF BIRTH
PARIS, FRANCE

DATE OF BIRTH 1971

WEBSITE
JOANAVASCONCELOS.
COM

Joana Vasconcelos describes herself as persevering, determined, hardworking, pragmatic and a little bit crazy. After studying at the António Arroio Art School, taking drawing courses at Ar.Co in Lisbon, a first-year design course at IADE University, then another course in jewelry and visual arts at Ar.Co, she set up a jewelry studio, which soon turned into a sculpture studio. Inspired in particular by everyday life, and more specifically by the symbols and objects that

surround us, she interprets the ordinary world in a way that generates new discourses and opinions.

Evoking the concept of ready-mades, the codes of new realism and pop culture, her works attempt to challenge contemporary reality by widening people's point of view: 'I believe that the objective of art is to lead individuals to question the world.' Her work is the result of a very personal journey,

Above:
Burlesque
110 × 160 × 50 cm
Hand-crocheted wool,
ornaments, polyester,
canvas, wooden and
stucco gilt frame,
plywood, 2014

Opposite:
Contamination
Variable dimensions
Hand-crocheted and
knitted wool, felt
appliqué, industrially
knitted fabric, fabrics,
ornaments, polystyrene,
polyester, steel
cables, 2008–10

Previous pages:
Pantelmina #1
176 × 1000 × 70 cm
Hand-knitted wool, industrially
knitted fabric, ratchet straps,
polyester, 2001

Above:
Big Booby #2
336 × 336 × 75 cm
Hand-crocheted wool,
industrially knitted fabrics,
polyester, stainless steel, 2011

and she claims not to be heavily influenced by other artists, except perhaps Louise Bourgeois, for her huge body of work and her long career ('I too will work as long as I live!') and Paula Rego, for her profound and detailed vision of the world of women, which mingles reality and the subconscious, fantasy and the notion of power, in a highly subversive way.

Joana was taught to crochet as a teenager by her grandmother but did not begin to use the technique seriously until 2001, with *Pantelmina #1* (pp. 116–17). This work is made up of a stuffed tube of multi-coloured knitting, ten metres long, attached to the wall by four purple straps. Seeing crochet as a technique that forms part of her nation's collective heritage, she uses it to fashion pieces that fit

Above:
True Faith
186 × 311 × 67 cm
Hand-crocheted wool, polyester, canvas, wooden and stucco gilt frame, plywood, 2014

Golden Valkyrie
650 × 1140 × 1360 cm
Hand-crocheted wool, industrially knitted
fabrics, fabrics, ornaments, polystyrene,
polyester, steel cables, 2012

together like jigsaw puzzles. She also alludes to the role of crochet lace in the historical isolation of Portuguese women; confined to their homes, unaware of their rightful places in the world of work, they passed on the technique to their daughters, thus perpetuating a suffocating form of oppression that lasted for four decades. Joana is attracted by the fact that lace can serve two purposes, being both a decorative object in itself and a textile that protects the surface of furniture. Because of the universal nature of the crochet hook, it can be found everywhere, from generation to generation, and is still prevalent in many Portuguese homes.

Crochet not only creates a variety of motifs and textures but also generates volume, allowing the artist to produce sculptural and even monumental pieces. Combining it with two other techniques, the craft of beaded embroidery, frequently found in northern Portugal, and the technology of sound and light, she creates works that challenge viewers with their size and high-tech nature. *Valkyrie Rán*, from the *Valkyries* series, created for the permanent collection of ARoS Aarhus Art Museum, is a 50-metre-long sculpture that spans the eight levels of the building. Powered by electricity, it is made up of crochet, fabric, ornaments, LED lights, microcontrollers, inflatable elements, steel cables and sound installations.

In 2005 Joana became known to a wider audience with her monumental work *The Bride*, exhibited at the Venice Biennnale. Five metres high, this chandelier made from 25,000 tampons is both majestic and full of minute details, combining ostentatious wealth, represented by the chandelier, with the femininity represented by the tampons that women normally keep hidden away. Virginal white contrasts with the absent red of menstrual blood.

Joana's huge sculptures are proof that crochet hooks can create true works of art. Like the artists of Nouveau Réalisme, she regularly chooses everyday objects and then transforms them, combining them (often wittily) and covering them with crochet lace to create strange, playful or disturbing scenes. The many roles of womanhood – warrior, wife, mother or housekeeper – are central to Joana's work, as she reinvents Portuguese traditions such as lace-making and ceramic tiles in order to compare and contrast the concepts of domination and submission, femininity and masculinity, strength and fragility.

Below:
The Island of Love
220 × 300 × 600 cm
Concrete statues, acrylic paint,
hand-crocheted cotton, plastic
globes, bulbs, electrical wiring, 2006

In June 2012 Joana took over the Château de Versailles and its gardens with her sculpture *Contamination* (p. 115), a patchwork of knitted tubes, tentacles and multicoloured stuffed shapes, first shown at the 2009 Venice Biennale and created using crochet, knitting and sewing. She was the first woman artist to exhibit her work at Versailles and more than 1.6 million visitors came to see her installation.

Joana always keeps a little notebook with her to jot down her meetings and sketch out ideas that come into her head, but she produces the works themselves entirely in the studio she has set up in a former warehouse in Lisbon, on the banks of the Tagus river. She has a team of about fifty people. Reflecting the size of her sculptures, her huge studio functions as a factory of art; it is piled high with fabrics, beads, crochet yarn and embroidery threads, with each element carefully arranged by colour, size and material, in an atmosphere of almost reverential calm.

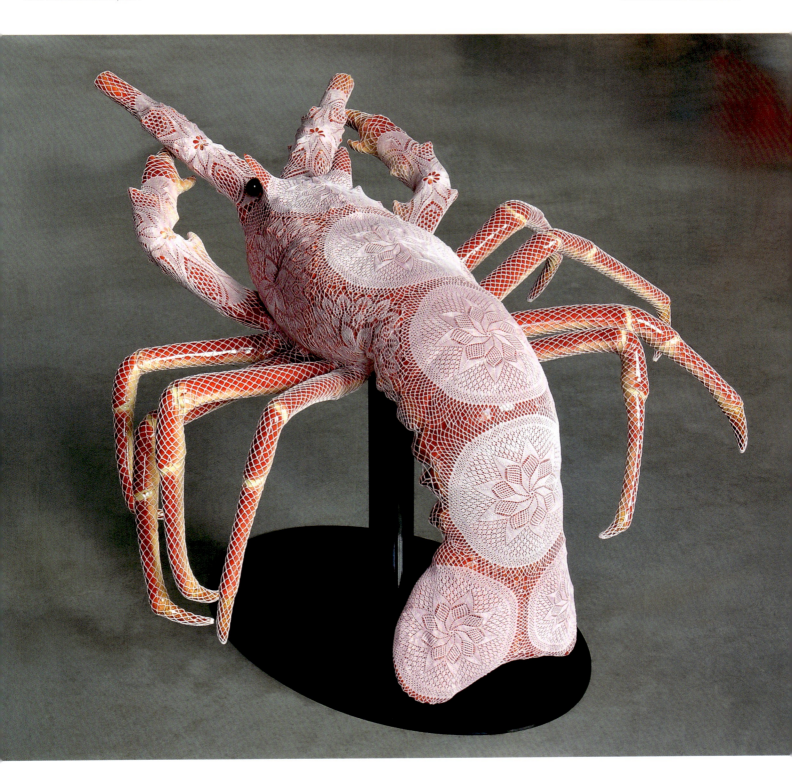

RANDI SAMSONSEN

PLACE OF RESIDENCE
TÓRSHAVN, FAROE ISLANDS

PLACE OF BIRTH
FAROE ISLANDS

DATE OF BIRTH
1977

WEBSITE
RANDISAMSONSEN. COM

Randi Samsonsen works with words, drawings and photographs without ever really knowing how her sculptures will turn out. 'To put it simply,' she says, 'you could say I start from nothing and then it turns into something.' Starting out from the raw yarn, which she cards herself, she tries to remain free and does not strive for any precise shape, while at the same time imposing rules on herself, one of which is a sense of unease. Letting go, not knowing how the end product will turn out while never feeling intimidated, even if the shape is becoming abstract and the work difficult: she experiences this feeling several times a day. She takes the time to be present in the moment, hoping that this approach will make her more patient, creative and open to others. By incorporating these elements into her work, she wants to share the sense of unease that lies within the finished work. It is a creative process that Pierre Soulages once described as: 'It's what I do that teaches me what I'm looking for.' Randi agrees with this statement, seeking to grow wiser and to question herself as an artist and a human being.

After studying textile design at the Danish Design School and the Steneby Art School in Sweden, Randi specialized in knitwear, exploring the processes of transforming yarn into surfaces and shapes. A course with Isabel Berglund, the Danish artist and textile designer, and a stint with Guðrun & Guðrun, a Faroese brand specializing in handmade clothing, completed her apprenticeship.

Above:
YELLOW // SECTIONS
(detail)
100 × 40 × 20 cm
Cotton, iron, 2014

She was only five years old when her grandmother taught her to knit and crochet. Young Randi proved very patient and applied herself, convinced that that it was essential to be able to turn yarn into useful objects if she was to become a good wife one day. Later, when she learned that knitting and crochet could serve as means of artistic expression, her childhood prejudices disappeared. She began to use wool as a student in her twenties, after meeting her first teacher of weaving, Tita Vinther, in the Faroe Islands. Having until then expressed herself in words, writing novels and short stories, she now changed her artistic approach. Her teacher noticed Randi's enthusiasm for working with yarn and encouraged her to follow this route and to pursue an artistic approach that incorporated weaving, knitting and crochet. Yarn gave her the language she was looking for. Since knitting and crochet had made up a large part of her education, it seemed like a good idea to use them in her art, drawing on their sculptural potential.

In her early works, she applied acrylic and watercolour paint to her knitted surfaces and objects. Nowadays she sometimes builds her

Far left and left:
Yellow
31 × 12 × 7 cm
Cotton, 2017

Neon
19 × 13 × 9 cm
Synthetics, 2017

Below left and right:
Untitled
20 × 21 × 13 cm and
12 × 13 × 13 cm
Cotton, 2017

work around metal or plastic objects, which then engage in a dialogue with the textile. The texture and flexibility of the yarn allow her to produce all kinds of different shapes, even though its elasticity and softness can often prove very challenging.

Her needles and crochet hooks (varying in size from 2.5 mm to 4 mm or more) give her a sense of freedom. Held in her hands, close to her body, they allow her to observe the progress of her pieces as their structure and form gradually emerge. The intensity and slow pace of the process force her to remain aware of the moment, her hands working at a rhythm that is always slower than that of her mind. She is fascinated by the way a length of yarn can be transformed into a three-dimensional form and enjoys the interaction between the material, the tool, the technique and herself. She believes that the sculpture starts to take on its own characteristics, she knows she is on the right path.

Randi Samsonsen creates as a means of expressing herself and communicating images, emotions and ideas, trying to provoke a reaction from viewers and open the possibility of dialogue. She constantly keeps moving on her artistic journey and does not

'I belong to the surrealist and abstract expressionist movements.'

Opposite:
No. 1
60 × 30 × 20 cm
Cotton, plastic
fishing float, 2015

believe any one of her works is
more important than the others,
except perhaps for *No. 1* (p. 127).
She feels a particular connection

Above:
Untitled
35 × 35 cm
Cotton, 2017

Opposite:
Untitled
150 × 150 cm
Cotton, mohair,
2013

with that piece of work and the tension that exists between the spherical form and the unruly organic growths surrounding it. It is almost

as though one were trying to break away from or dominate the other.
This composition, created at a time when she herself was struggling
to accept and understand change following an illness in her family,
reflects a desire to reconcile the known and the unknown, calmness
and noise. She says she was trying to express her confused feelings
without making the circumstances directly visible.

FRANÇOISE TELLIER-LOUMAGNE

PLACE OF RESIDENCE
FRANCONVILLE AND
MARCIAC, FRANCE

PLACE OF BIRTH
**GENNEVILLIERS,
FRANCE**

DATE OF BIRTH **1948**

WEBSITE
**FRANÇOISE-TELLIER-
LOUMAGNE.COM**

Member of the Ateliers
d'Art de France

Françoise Tellier-Loumagne discovered textile making at ESAA Duperré college of art and design in Paris in the late 1960s. Since then, she has looked for ways to express herself in sculptural 2D and 3D forms, using textiles, stainless steel, bricks and pebbles and applying a variety of techniques. The works she has created, which are regularly displayed in schools, exhibitions and books, are often based on the theme of nature. Influenced by painting, sculpture and contemporary architecture, as well as by current fashion, she is fuelled by a mass of eclectic information but tries to avoid clichés.

While nature remains fundamental to her art, she is also inspired by a variety of locations, such as empty attics, for which she has created some twenty site-specific works. She has also written a book on

Above:
Cube
Each side 32 cm
Simulated stocking stitch
Metal frame, chain
stitch embroidery in yarn
made from wool fabric,
printed polyester and
cotton, 2012

Opposite:
Amphorae
Height 6–54 cm
Glass and ceramic
sheathed in wool fabric,
crochet, knitting, 2011

Opposite:
Mosaic
96 × 106 cm
Little cushions knitted
from cotton braid, in
purl stitch and fancy
ribbing, 2014

Françoise does not talk about her work much; she prefers to illustrate and explain it in her books** on the techniques of knitting, felting, embroidery and textile design, as an extension of her role as a teacher of textile design at many French institutions, including ESAA Duperré, ENSAAMA Olivier de Serres, ESAAT in Roubaix, and La Martinière-Diderot in Lyon, as well as schools in Canada, Germany, Switzerland and Mongolia.

After concentrating for some ten years on crochet and knitting, preferring to use pure new wool, cotton and silk, as well as viscose, lurex and metal, she now feels she knows these techniques too well. Rather than leaving them behind, however, she revisits them occasionally, often drawn by the sensuality of the colours and materials, and enjoying the way that the flexibility of the stitches allows them to be moulded and transformed, producing a multitude of different textures, opacities and motifs.

After exhibiting her textile work widely, Françoise has now been working for some time on pieces that are more sculptural and closer to industrial art. Her graphic works always have a strong impact, whether they are sparse or complex, neutral or colourful, deep black or pure white, saturated or fluorescent, ethereal and fragile or monumental and heavy, gossamer-like or organic. Her work can be appreciated close up or from a distance, in vast indoor and outdoor spaces, organically expanding across all kinds of surfaces.

1,000 ways of being creative,* listing a huge number of techniques, states of mind, processes and influences. She hopes that, as a result, others may recognize themselves in her works, an idea that lies at the very heart of her artistic approach.

She learned to knit at the age of ten, taught by an aunt who loved knitting, then discovered crochet at a school of applied arts during physics and chemistry lessons: 'Patchwork ponchos were in fashion at the time.' She likes to work with simple straight yarn but also uses all kinds of fancy yarns that she collects or manufactures herself, like the thick rope-like strands she is currently using, fashioned from woollen fabric or printed cotton. Although she prefers to work with 2–3.5 mm needles because they are easy to handle, she does use larger ones (10–25 mm) if need be. Her crochet hooks range in size from 0.75 to 25 mm.

The pleasure and necessity of expressing herself led her to begin creating, fascinated by the process itself and organizing her work in order to ensure that the time required to finish a piece is as efficiently managed as possible. She is constantly researching different subjects and works on several projects at the same time: 'I progress mainly piece by piece in my work, mostly in my spare time…'

Above:
Simulated Stitches
c. 70 × 70 cm
Wool fabric relief
made using sewing
techniques: darts
and gathers, 2013

* *1,000 manières de créer* (2010), published by Éditions de La Martinière, Paris.
** *The Art of Knitting* (2005), *The Art of Embroidery* (2006) and *The Art of Felt* (2008), published by Thames & Hudson, London.

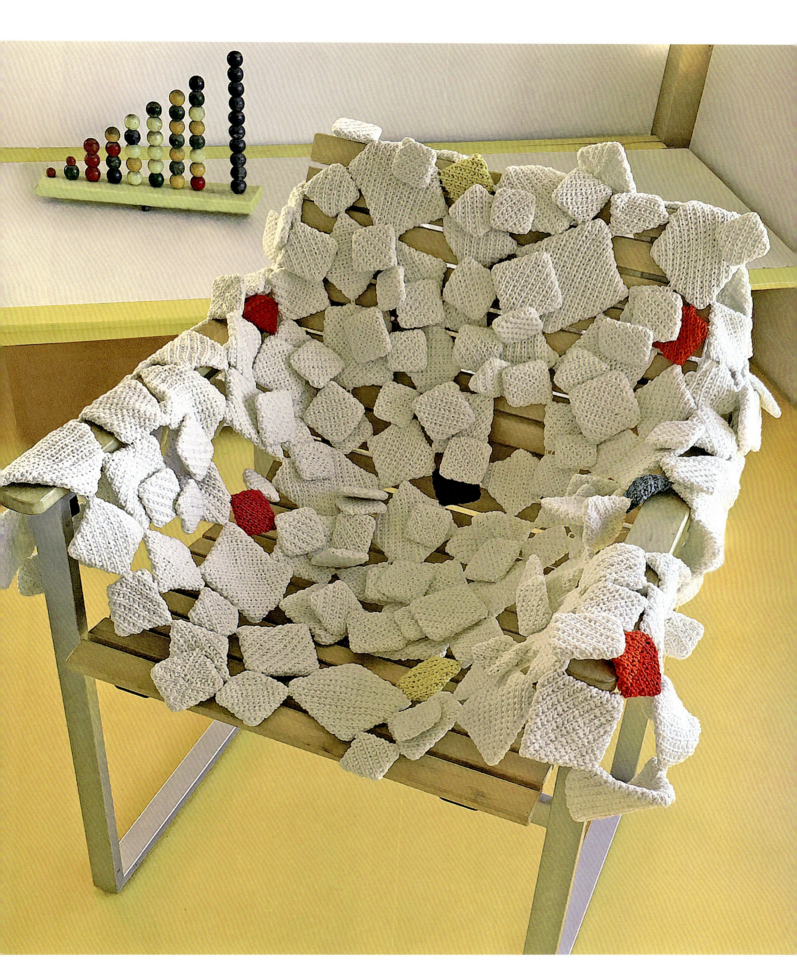

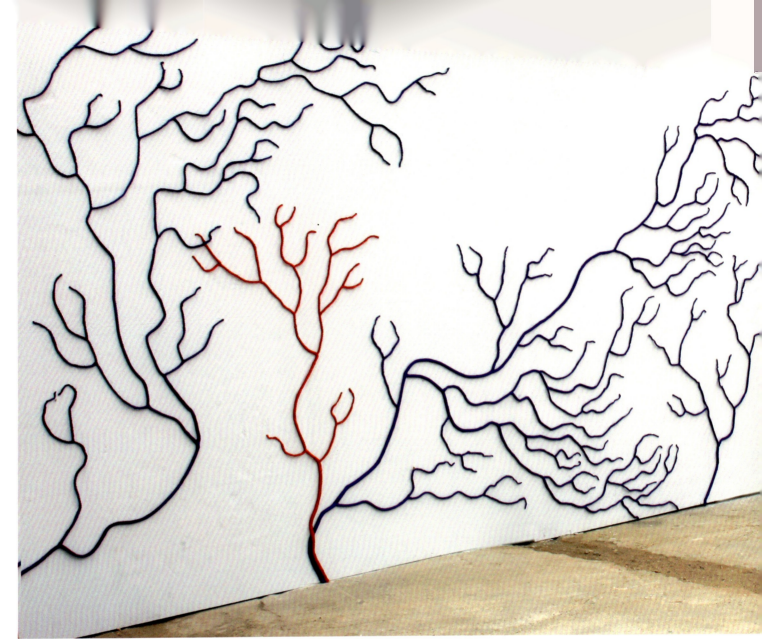

BEN CUEVAS

PLACE OF RESIDENCE
LOS ANGELES, USA

PLACE OF BIRTH
RIVERSIDE, CALIFORNIA, USA

DATE OF BIRTH **1987**

WEBSITE
BENCUEVAS.COM

Although Ben Cuevas uses a wide range of techniques that include sculpture, installation, performance, photography and video, knitting remains central to his work. His roots are varied – Spanish and Puerto Rican on his father's side, Jewish, German, Russian and Polish on his mother's – and the notion of identity lies at the heart of his work. Identifying as a queer and HIV-positive artist, Ben regards knitting as a meditative activity that can explore and challenge the sexist ideologies inherent in this medium.

He studied art at Hampshire College in Amherst, Massachusetts, graduating in 2005, and learned to knit thanks to his great friend Jessica Ruvalcaba. At first he knitted to pass the time and meditate but when Jessica taught him how to make a hat, he realized that the technique would allow him to produce any form he wanted. Passionately interested in the body and anatomy, he then began to knit a human heart, creating his first sculpture in wool. Later, while

Above and left:
Knit Veins:
Fiber of Our Being
12 × 3.65 m, 2013

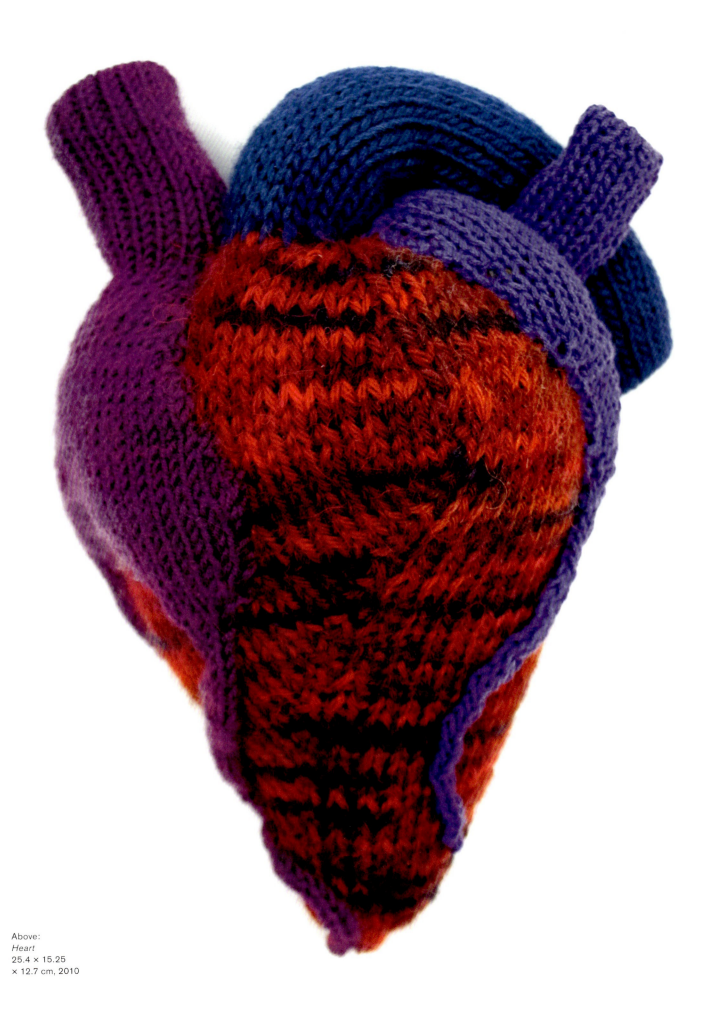

Above:
Heart
25.4 × 15.25
× 12.7 cm, 2010

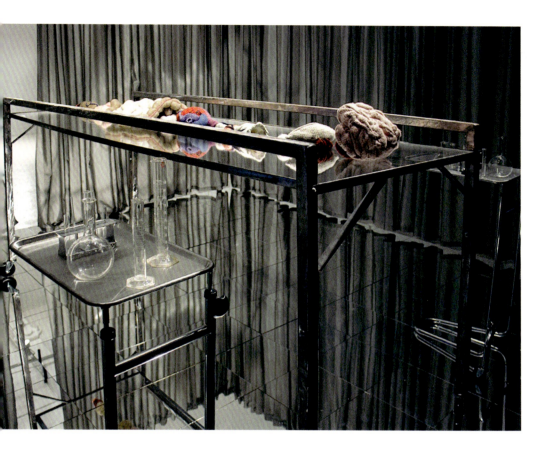

studying performance art and photography, he decided to broaden the use of knitting and apply it to performance art, making playful use of its feminine connotations. In the 2014 performance piece *Jockstrap*, he sat naked in a men's locker room and knitted himself a jockstrap from start to finish. In order to highlight the sexism stereotypically inherent in knitting, he contrasted it with the masculine image of underwear for sportsmen, and set the work within the macho atmosphere of a locker room.

From politics to metaphysics, his work is inspired by feminist ideologies, pop culture and the concept of the human mind and body, with blood playing a symbolic role: 'it is the bringer of both life and death.' In *Knit Veins: Fiber of Our Being* (pp. 134–35), he challenges the public's fear of HIV and tries to reintegrate queer culture into the social body. He does the same in *Ghosts of the Trucks of the West Side Highway*, a work in which he commemorates the 'sex trucks' that once parked beneath the West Side Highway in New York in the 1970s. An admirer of the works of the gay artist and militant campaigner David Wojnarowicz, and of Ron Athey, famous for his extreme and bloody physical performances, Ben created an alter ego for himself, called *BenBot 5000*, whose fictional career as an

Above:
The Hospital Room
490 × 490 × 365 cm,
2010

Right, from top
to bottom:
Brain
30.5 × 30.5 ×
30.5 cm, 2010

3rd Eye
30.5 × 30.5 ×
7.6 cm, 2010

Thyroid
30.5 × 12.7 ×
7.6 cm, 2010

Heart
25.4 × 15.25 ×
12.7 cm, 2010

Intestines
45.7 × 50.8 ×
10.15 cm, 2010

Genitosexual
30.5 × 17.8 ×
7.6 cm, 2010

Rectum
30.5 × 10.15 ×
10.15 cm, 2010

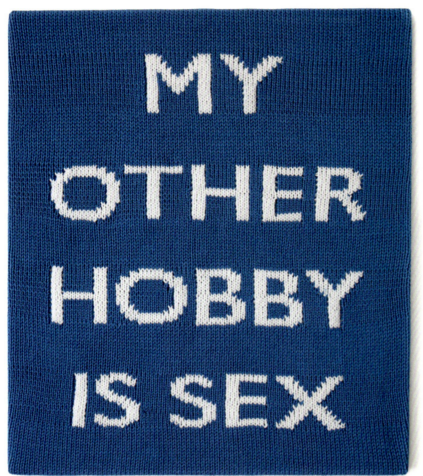

'I love the moment right before you finish a piece, when it is becoming what you envisioned and you can see the light at the end of the tunnel.'

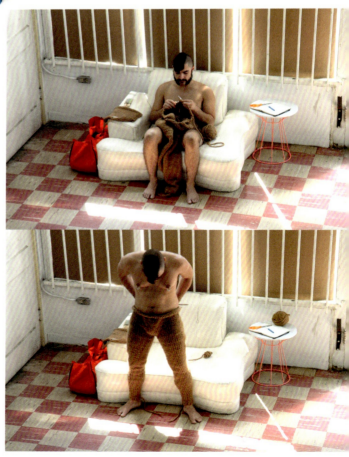

intergalactic rockstar, as discussed in a fake interview with *Rolling Stone* magazine, enabled him to explore his favourite themes in a digital context. This exploration of online identity and pop culture also led to *The Tweetables Series: Knit Text in 140 Characters or Less* (above), a series of wall hangings that combine contemporary language, a social media aesthetic and the anachronistic softness of knitted yarn: 'Throughout its pluralities, I see my work as reflecting the condition of embodiment, exploring the intersections of the mind and body, what it means to have a body, to inhabit a body, to be a body incarnated in and interacting with the world.'

Transcending the Material is a multimedia installation created and in 2010 when Ben was an artist in residence at the Wassaic Project, an arts collective and residency programme in Wassaic, New York. A knitted human skeleton is seated on a pyramid of Borden's condensed milk cans. Above it, screen prints on Plexiglas are suspended from the ceiling. The installation was a reference to material culture and the local history of Wassaic, where the Borden factory was based for many years, but also invites the viewer to meditate on the

Left:
Duality No. 1
Masculine / Feminine
106 × 183 ×
91.5 cm, 2013

Right:
*Anatomical
Knit Hoods*
25.5 × 25.5 ×
22.8 cm, 2011

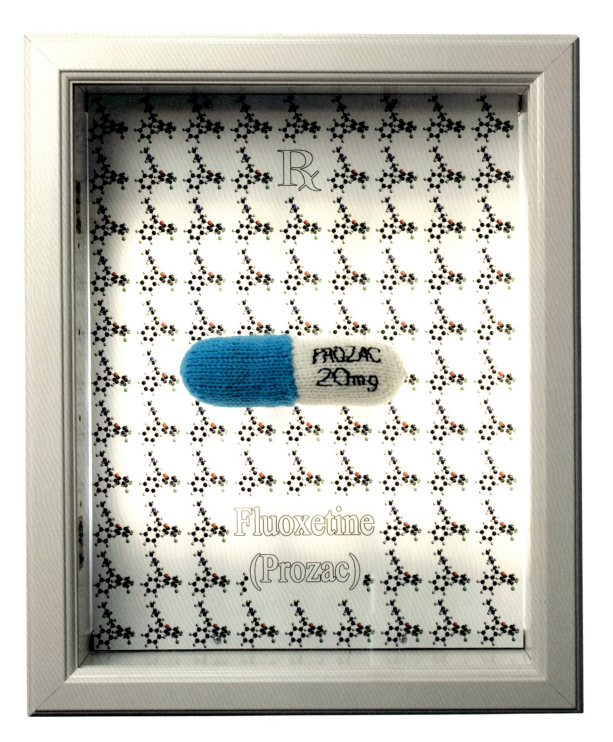

Left and opposite, above:
Medicine Cabinets
31 × 49 × 12.7 cm, 2010

Below:
Knit PrEP
15.25 × 6.35
× 5 cm, 2014

question of transcendence, on what lies beyond the perceptible, and on the possibilities of the intelligible.

Playing with connotations of gender and blurring the lines between the arts and crafts, Ben Cuevas uses wool for its symbolism and its ability to give shape to his projects, using needles of varying sizes according to need and preferring to work with 100% natural Cascade yarn.

CLÉMENCE JOLY

PLACE OF RESIDENCE
PARIS, FRANCE

PLACE OF BIRTH
IVRY-SUR-SEINE, FRANCE

DATE OF BIRTH **1986**

WEBSITE
CLEMENCEJOLY.COM

A creative Parisian in her thirties, Clémence Joly reproduces ordinary objects in wool, drawing her inspiration from the world around her. She doesn't seek out anything in particular, but is open to all kinds of inspiration for future projects, for instance from materials or shapes. She may be attracted by an exhibition, crowds on the street and in the Metro, exotic market stalls with their displays of unusual fruit, haberdasheries, hobby shops or DIY stores.

A graphic designer by training, she studied at ENSAAMA Olivier de Serres in Paris and then gained an MA in graphic communication and design at Central Saint Martins in London. She has been working freelance since 2000, focusing on brand identities, signage and museum graphics: 'I love graphic design, the book as an object, paper, typography, motifs.' She has worked in crochet since her MA, both for herself and for clients. In 2008 she first combined the subjects of meat and textiles at Central Saint Martins. Having come up with the idea of creating hybrid objects linking the two realms, she decided that she wanted to make a woollen roast, and asked her mother to teach her to crochet. The discovery of this medium proved a revelation: 'I went to a London shop that sold wool and suggested setting up knitting and crochet classes. The manager gave me one month and carte blanche to create a window display for her shop.' Her collection of crocheted meat then began to grow, ending up as *The Wool Butchery*. Since then,

Above:
In Cold Water
Langoustine, wool, 2017

Opposite:
An Eye for an Eye
Cotton, wadding, 2016

she has continued to enlarge her diverse range of crochet subjects.

She loves the work of Joana Vasconcelos (see p. 114), and also admires the 'crochet taxidermy' of Shauna Richardson, the eccentrically distorted objects of Sarah Illenberger, the crochet work of Aurélie Mathigot (p. 212)

Above:
English Breakfast
for New Look
Wool, cotton,
wadding, 2010

and Anne-Claire Petit, the textile sculptures and embroideries of Louise Bourgeois and the controversial works of Tracey Emin.

Clémence says that wool makes objects soft, witty and inoffensive, radically changing their original context: 'A woollen roast is useless and unusual, it stands out, it no longer oozes blood.' What she likes most is the discrepancy between the object's lifelike appearance and

Above:
*Roast – The
Wool Butchery*
Alpaca wool, cotton,
wadding, 2009

Left:
*Sliced Sausage –
The Wool Butchery*
Wool, cotton,
wadding, 2011

Overleaf:
*Display – The
Wool Butchery*
Wool, cotton,
wadding, 2009–12

its lack of purpose. The idea of wrapping things in wool, which is more traditionally used to cover the body, pleases her.

Although the technique requires great patience, crocheting allows her to undo and redo things. As long as the work is still unfinished, errors are allowed: 'The multitude of yarns and stitches mean you can recreate anything.'

Alternating between tiny crochet hooks and very large ones, Clémence works with any material that catches her eye, attracted by colour and texture. She works with plastic laces, rubber, wire, chain, even seaweed, and sees no limits to her creativity. When images of objects spontaneously spring into her mind, she immediately wants to touch them and turn them into reality, because until she has handled a thing, she does not feel that it exists. It is almost as if she had eyes at her fingertips: 'I read somewhere that an idea that has not been made real does not exist. And I want my ideas to exist.'

She recently worked on a set of Christmas window displays of the Bon Marché department store, creating more than 140 figures in the form of snowballs adorned with little bird-like feet. It was a big job but she loved completing it and it gave her the chance to cooperate with a team of set designers, animators and lighting engineers.

Clémence is currently working on the subject of snakes: the project combines taxidermy, reptiles, colour and entomological cases: 'All these things draw my attention; I find them beautiful.'

FLOCONS ENSEMBLE !

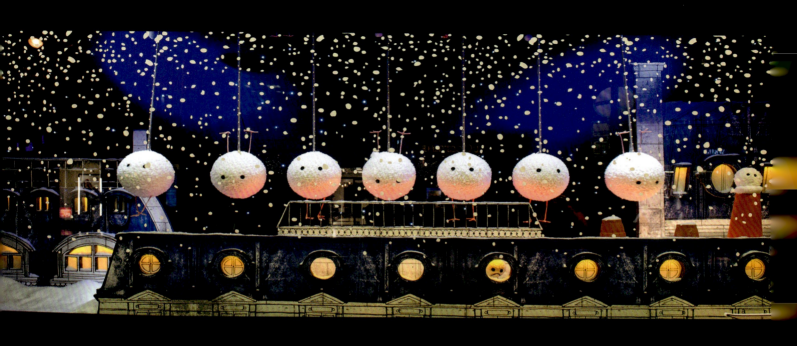

#ILNEIGERIVEGAUCHE

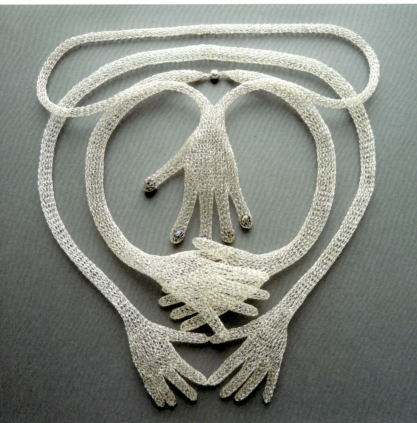

BLANKA
ŠPERKOVÁ

PLACE OF RESIDENCE
BRNO, CZECH REPUBLIC

PLACE OF BIRTH
**BANSKÁ BYSTRICA,
SLOVAKIA**

DATE OF BIRTH **1948**

WEBSITE
**BLANKASPERKOVA.
AMANITA-DESIGN.NET**

After studying graphic design at the School of Applied Arts in Bratislava, followed by a course at the Prague School of Applied Arts, where she studied the arts of animation and puppetry, Blanka Šperková taught herself to work with wire. Although inspired by the traditional craft techniques of the Roma people of Slovakia, she uses a different method: the technique of finger crochet. She starts off with a basic loop and creates both sculptures and jewelry. At the beginning of her career, she designed figurative forms based on the human body and animal motifs but eventually these forms evolved and became more abstract.

Above:
Hands Necklaces
Finger crochet, silver-plated wire, 2000

Right:
Three Coloured Necklaces
Finger crochet, metallic wires varnished in different colours, 2012

150

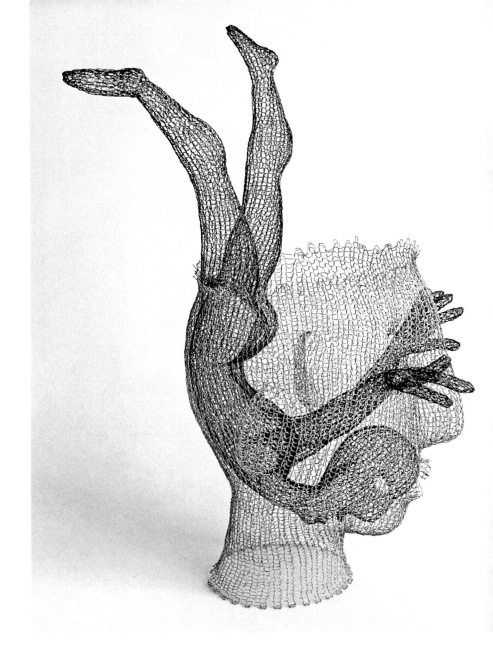

'Despite my attempts to avoid direct similarities, the concrete forms that emerge always suggest something familiar.'

After spending years making heads, hands, legs, torsos, backs and fronts, she began to produce less figurative forms, although always with an organic component. Her objects seem to take on a life of their own, spontaneously bringing themselves into being. Matter becomes form, or form becomes matter. 'Tiny shifts can appear right at the start and then go on growing, becoming bigger, changing the scale in time and space': these words, which she came across in a book, intrigued her because they described just what she was trying to do through her work. She works on different scales, letting the diameter of the wire determine the size of the loops, which itself dictates the final volume of the piece: 'If I do not respect the dictates of the structure, the form loses its internal tension, its power. It dries up, like an apple without its juice.' Manipulating the airy transparency of the crocheted wire, she builds forms that explore the interplay of light and shade.

Her work is inspired by the traditional 18th- and 19th-century crafts of the Roma people of Slovakia, in particular by their method of repairing ceramics and broken pots. This unique technique consisted of strengthening the pots with wire. The tough nature of this work meant that it was reserved for men, whose hands were more resistant to the lacerations caused by the wire.

In her desire to understand how the Roma worked with this material, Blanka Šperková began to use fine wire and discovered something unexpected: to avoid loose ends of wire, she had to loop the length of wire through itself with her fingers, which made the

Above:
Through the Head
40 × 30 × 20 cm
Finger crochet,
stainless steel wire,
1985

structure look as though it were knitted, while its transparency recalled lacework. Originating from a region of Slovakia where lacemaking was still considered a feminine craft, she combines the toughness of a traditionally male occupation with the delicacy of women's work. Sometimes she flattens the objects she produces and uses them to make black and white prints; sometimes the 3D shapes are turned into painstakingly animated films. She likes to use projectors to create shadows that loom over her objects and make them more expressive; one such example was her installation *Tao Lace*, featuring rooms lit by projectors that were activated randomly by a computer, creating evanescent lace-like shadows that moved across the wall. Wanting to take this experiment further, Blanka now makes her objects turn at random, so that the shadows they project appear even more unearthly.

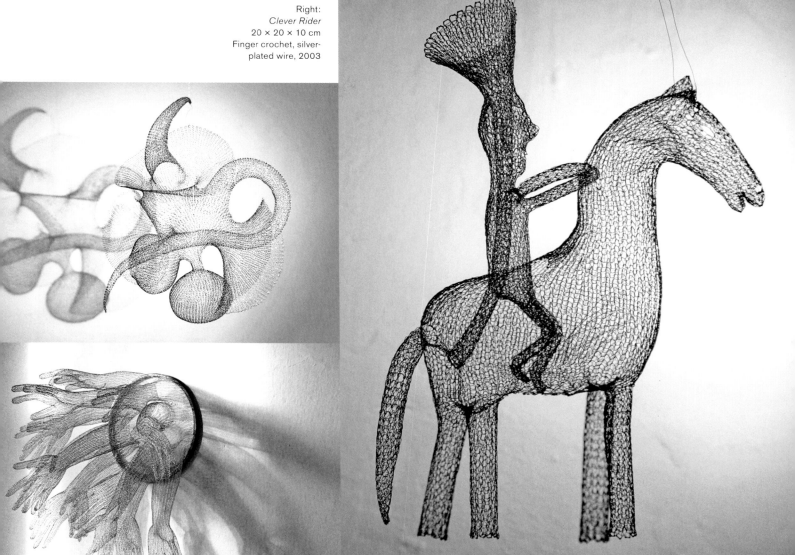

Right:
Clever Rider
20 × 20 × 10 cm
Finger crochet, silver-
plated wire, 2003

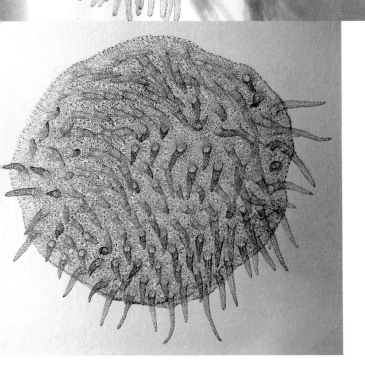

Above left:
Two Ends
50 × 50 × 50 cm
Finger crochet, stainless
steel wire, 2005

Centre left:
Begging Hands
55 × 55 × 55 cm
Finger crochet, stainless
steel wire, 1986

Below left:
Pillow
40 × 60 × 20 cm
Finger crochet, stainless
steel wire, 2004

Overleaf, left:
Jellyfish
50 × 50 × 50 cm
Finger crochet, stainless
steel wire, 2010

Overleaf, right:
Bird Which Ate The Plastic
60 × 60 × 40 cm
Finger crochet, stainless steel
wire and metallic wire varnished
in different colours, 2013

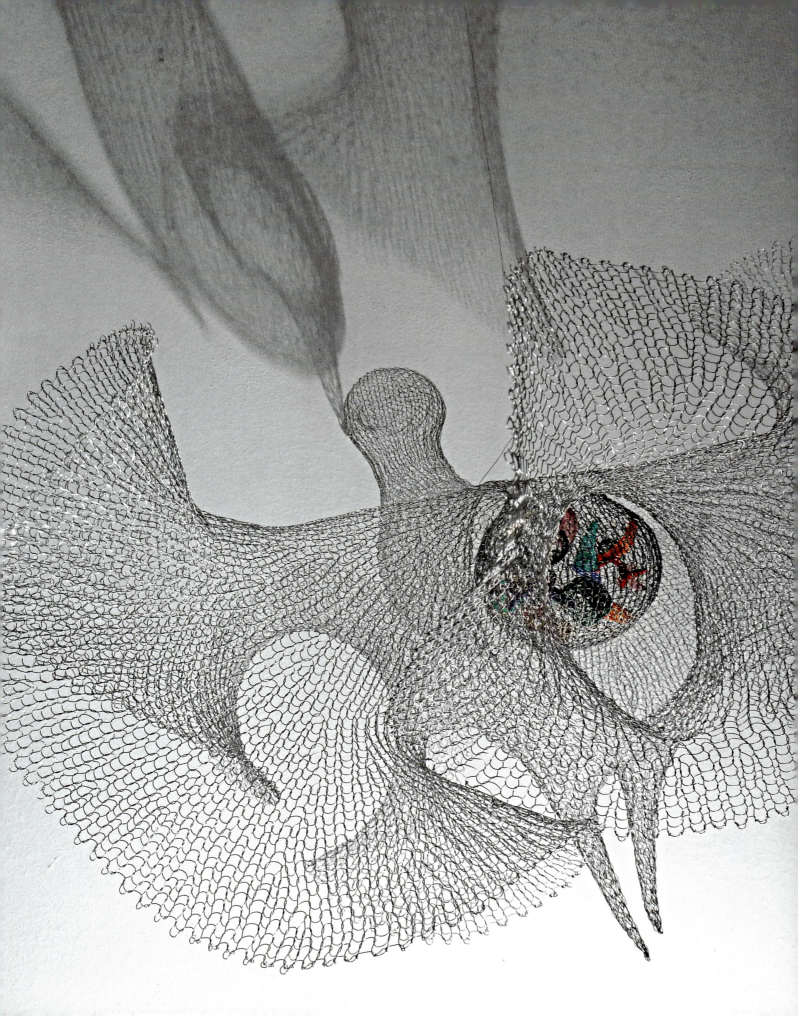

MARIE BERGSTEDT

PLACE OF RESIDENCE
SAN FRANCISCO, USA

PLACE OF BIRTH
KALAMAZOO,
MICHIGAN, USA

DATE OF BIRTH 1944

WEBSITE
MARIEBERGSTEDTARTIST.
COM

Marie Bergstedt grew up shuttling back and forth between her foster parents, her biological mother and three different fathers, her dog and her tricycle. By studying the theme of the family unit, its internal relationships and also relationships with friends, she wants to draw attention to the way each person plays a role in the life of others. As a genuine reflection of her philosopher, her work is inspired by her unhappy experiences but transforms them into something positive. She wants her viewers to be able to identify with her work, to read their own stories in it and to learn to move beyond their own pain.

Above left:
Summer
102 × 32 × 2.5 cm
Crochet, knitting and sewing: cotton, mohair, angora, buttons, canvas, 2012

Above centre:
Kitchen Companion
38 × 30 × 11 cm
Crocheted cotton and buttons, various yarns, 2010

Above right:
Eighteen
142 × 61 × 5 cm
Crochet, knitting and sewing, cotton yarns, buttons on canvas, 2013

After spending most of her life as head of development for non-profit organizations, Marie now works full time as an artist. After leaving school, she took a number of courses and worked in studios across the USA, studying art at Wright State University, Ohio, and then at the San Francisco Art Institute. Constantly on the move as she followed her husband all over the USA, she never spent long enough at the universities and art schools of California, Ohio and Illinois to obtain a degree. After finishing her studies, she specialized in photography and began to tell stories through her photographs, while at the same time continuing to make clothes and jewelry.

Above left and right:
Victoria Red
114 × 61 × 6.5 cm
Crochet, knitting and sewing; cotton, mohair, wool, silk, recycled wedding-dress fabric, necklace, buttons and beads on canvas, 2014

She learned to crochet and sold her first small pieces at the age of eight, then took up embroidery. A few years later, she learned to knit at a 4-H club run by the US Department of Agriculture whose mission was to turn youths from rural areas into responsible citizens. Throughout her life, Marie has never stopped knitting and crocheting, inspired by her great aunt and her grandmother who were great knitters and made such an indelible mark on her life that she has dedicated some of her works to them. But it was when she discovered the fibre sculptures of Carol Beadle, a textile artist and teacher, that she had a revelation: knitting and crochet seemed to her to be an ideal means of artistic expression.

Her work is based mainly on her personal experiences and she uses knitting and crochet to add meaning to her message, via their

*'When knitting and crochet cannot express
what is in my mind, I use other techniques.'*

Left:
Countdown
41 × 99 × 25 cm
Crochet over aluminium
wire, cotton, 2008

associations with the concepts of tradition and memory. Her pieces are also a means of honouring the people who are her main subjects. *Mikey of Mallory*, for example, is a tribute to her homeless brother, who lives on the streets in Key West, Florida, while her series of telephones (p. 156) is a reference to her foster mother.

She uses wool to achieve a felted effect, and exploits crochet's ability to take on any form as a basis for her sculptures; she enjoys combining the textures of different fibres and stitches and loves the palette of colours that yarn can offer. Indeed, she often dyes her own yarn to obtain a particular colour.

Using found objects, painting, sculpture, photography, printing and also drawing, she has been creating art since the age of eleven, with knitting and crochet playing a major role. Viewers never see the paintings that lie beneath her work, the photographs she took to give her ideas, or the collages and sketches she made in order get the image she wants.

Once she has thought up and planned a project she moves on to making it, always afraid it might not turn out as she wants. Then come the long and often tiring hours of labour. She says that she tries to think of other things to avoid getting bored, listening to audio books and thinking about how the various pieces should be put together, given that none of her works follow the same rules. A piece might take off in several directions over the course of the process, but unravelled and reknitted when required, it will eventually be completed to her satisfaction when all the issues she has encountered during its making are finally resolved.

Left:
Triker
Girl: 81 × 36 × 33 cm
Tricycle: 61 × 66 × 53 cm
Crochet, sewing; cotton, buttons,
recycled tricycle, old doilies, 2009

JESSICA DANCE

PLACE OF RESIDENCE
LONDON, UK

PLACE OF BIRTH
WINCHESTER, UK

DATE OF BIRTH **1988**

WEBSITE
JESSICADANCE.COM

Jessica Dance is a textile artist who draws her inspiration from observing and reinterpreting items and experiences from everyday life. Whether it's a typical meal, a telephone, a luxury handbag or a vintage computer, she wants to remind us how attached we are to these objects and to challenge the price we are prepared to pay in order to have them.

After graduating in fashion, Jessica set up a business producing models and props for publishers and advertising. At first she made most of her projects from paper, but soon decided to explore other materials in order to move her work in a more personal direction. She then began to experiment with making fabrics. Although she enjoyed the process, she wanted to have more control over the appearance, texture and colour of her work and so decided to learn machine knitting.

Combining crafts with contemporary art, Jessica also works for major brands, magazines including *Tatler* and *Stylist*, for whom she

Above:
Knit Nikes
Life size
Lambswool, 2016

Opposite:
*Louis Vuitton
Camera Box Bag* (for
Stylist magazine)
Life size
Lambswool, 2016

Previous pages:
Jessica Dance × Jon Burgerman
Characters designed by Jon Burgerman
Life size, 2017

Below:
Motorola DynaTAC 8000X
Life size
Lambswool, 2016

produced knitted replicas of pieces from the autumn/winter 2016 fashion collections, and for ITV television, for whom she made key props and elements for an ad break featuring knitted remakes of six existing commercials.

She enjoys the challenge of starting with an idea and then creating very detailed pieces that take hours of work, trial and error and retouching, stages that she regards as an integral part of the creative process. Once she has decided on a subject, she spends some time researching and refining the concept, sketching freehand and exploring different paths, until she finds a design that matches what she wants. She then moves on to producing it in three dimensions.

Since 2012, the year she first taught herself to knit, Jessica has been drawn to the process itself, which she finds highly satisfying as it gives her the feeling of creating something from a simple strand of wool. A natural yarn that is environmently friendly, wool is both very solid and very flexible, as well as being pleasing to work with. Jessica likes the idea of introducing a material usually associated with fashion and interior decoration into the world of contemporary art. Her knitted replica of the Camera Box bag (p. 161) by the famous fashion house of Louis Vuitton proved particularly complex and therefore needed a great deal of preparation. But although every piece is time-consuming and always involves making mistakes, she loves the stage of putting the finishing touches to an object and finds the moment the work is completed particularly gratifying.

Opposite:
Apple Macintosh 128K
Life size
Lambswool, 2016

Overleaf, left and right:
Comfort Food
Life size
Lambswool, 2014

NATHAN VINCENT

PLACE OF RESIDENCE
LOS ANGELES, USA

PLACE OF BIRTH
**MUSKEGON,
MICHIGAN, USA**

DATE OF BIRTH **1981**

WEBSITE
NATHANVINCENT.COM

The son of a preacher, Nathan Vincent had a very traditional upbringing and says that although he was cherished and cosseted, he was also often scolded. Growing up under the watchful eyes of his father's congregation, he felt uncomfortable in his own skin and worried about what others thought about him, what he did and how he looked. Although he'd been taught that it was a sin to be gay and pointless to become an artist, he was nonetheless eventually able to embrace his sexual orientation and make art for a living. Although his status as a

Above and right:
Let's Play War!
installation
Variable dimensions
Yarn, foam, cotton
fabric, textile hardener,
steel, 2015

Above and right:
Locker Room
installation
Lion brand wool,
foam, wood, 2011

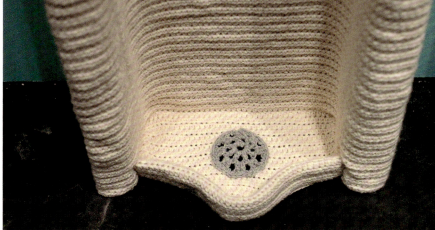

preacher's son caused him pain during his childhood, it also helped him to become a strong adult, sure of what he is and what he wants out of life.

After five years at university, where he concentrated on drawing and painting, he realised that these techniques would not be much use to him if he wanted to produce sincere and original works. Crochet, which he had learned as a child, seemed to him to be best suited to his purpose because of its authenticity. One day he was visiting a friend who was knitting a sweater, without a pattern, turning her work again and again instead of casting on row by row. While watching her knit, he realized that she was working in three dimensions instead of two; for the first time he saw how the world of yarn could be linked to the world of sculpture. But the real inspiration that led him to work with yarn came when he discovered the art of the Egyptian-born Ghada Amer. This embroidery artist is concerned with femininity, redefining and regaining power. Her large-scale embroideries, which at first sight look like paintings but are actually made up of coloured threads, together with her use of erotic imagery and the way that she allows trailing threads to distort her figures, affected him deeply.

His earliest works were inspired by childhood memories: of his uncles who liked hunting and bodybuilding, his father who never let go of his briefcase, his grandfather seated on his reclining armchair, his 'throne', watching TV, his friends' fathers, the farmers and the handymen. These examples came from from close to home and reinforced stereotypes about gender and about what boys were allowed to do. Nathan Vincent began to use crochet in his work because of its automatic feminine associations. Where he came from, needlework was only for women. If men ever started to crochet or knit they would be regarded as 'queer', which was the ultimate taboo for a young boy from a conservative Christian background. Torn between the desire to crochet and the feeling that he ought to hide his interest in this sort of pastime to protect his social identity, he realized that creating

'Much of what I was trying to achieve with these techniques had already been done before.'

Right:
*Don't Make Me
Count to Three!*
Wool, wood,
cardboard, 2013

Left:
Threat II
Wool, glass fibre, 2013

Below:
Brass Knuckles
Wool, metal rings, 2013

typically masculine objects using a process regarded as intrinsically feminine could help him raise the issue of gender and express himself in a simple way that everybody could understand. He says that over time, he came to see how ridiculous this taboo was. Since we are all human beings capable of so many things, he wondered why he was restricting himself to activities assigned to his sex. Deeply involved in the art world and also the growing craft movement born out of the rejection of digital domination, he is also very committed to LGBT issues and continues to explore them in his work.

He prefers to crochet rather than knit his sculptures, loving the three-dimensionality of crochet. Knitting may be perfect for making flat pieces or hangings, but it requires more advance planning (because it is done with multiple live stitches) while crochet allows you to work on one stitch at a time, which frees your mind and allows for greater spontaneity and creativity. Nathan works with a variety of different crochet hooks. He mainly uses acrylic fibre and very rarely wool, allowing his technique to evolve as new ideas emerge: tiny hooks for delicate doilies, large hooks for more imposing works. He has even worked with an S-shaped meat hook.

Of all the stages in the process, Nathan prefers the beginning and the end. He finds the initial stage of creation stimulating and motivating, when he has an idea in mind and wants to see it made real. Then comes the difficult and often boring stage, involving hours of repeating the same motions, while dealing with any problems that arise. Finally, the last stage comes, when the piece takes on its final form. That is when he has a sudden sense of pleasure and is keen to

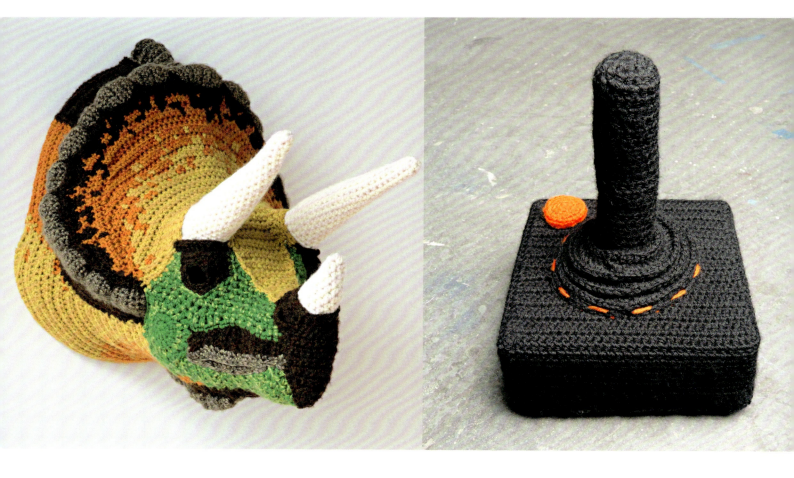

see it finished. He shapes his sculptures in various ways: some pieces are self-supporting, while others are stuffed with wool or cotton, or filled by an armature of foam. He says it all depends on what he wants to achieve in the end.

Whether he is in his studio, strewn with bits of yarn that tend to stick to his clothes, or on a plane, in a museum, on the sofa, in a park, a shop or even a bar, he is always crocheting, and likes to do so visibly, in public. He explores any idea that piques his curiosity and seizes any opportunity that presents itself, driven by the pleasure of creating and always hoping that his finished pieces will interact with the public. Although it's not his main motivation for working, he says that he loves to see people looking at his art.

EMMANUELLE BARRÈRE

PLACE OF RESIDENCE
BERLIN, GERMANY

PLACE OF BIRTH
NICE, FRANCE

DATE OF BIRTH **1979**

WEBSITE
**EMMANUELLE-ESTHER.
TUMBLR.COM**

Thanks to a father who worked as a furniture upholsterer and a mother trained as a seamstress, Emmanuelle Barrère became an enthusiastic crafter. She learned to knit from her grandmother at the age of eight, then sold wool and advised customers in La Droguerie, a craft store in Nice, for two years: 'I was working twelve hours a week and there was only one thing I wanted: to go home and knit all the ideas

Above:
Untitled
Wool, mohair,
alpaca, angora,
2014

176

Left:
Untitled
30% wool, 70% synthetic,
2015

Right:
Guerlain
Length 9 m,
circumference 10 cm
55% wool, 45%
synthetic, 2016

that had come into my head during the day.' After getting a qualification in social work – 'it's not connected with it, but ultimately my interest in people has helped me a lot in my career' – she enrolled in fashion school.

Taking her inspiration from everyday life, she reinterprets reality with a preference for the simplest of ideas, which she often regards as the most beautiful. Drawn to the idea of making a piece stitch by stitch, she loves the slow pace and the time it takes to create something: 'It is important to show that you have to take time to do things.' Emmanuelle loves yarns, colours and materials, especially wool, as well as all the shapes and stitches that knitting allows.

She admires the work of Sandra Backlund, a Swedish fashion designer known for her sculptural knits, and is deeply impressed by the exaggerated female forms and unusual proportions that give Backlund's creations their futuristic look.

Driven by the pleasure of seeing her ideas come to life, she pulls them out of her head and makes them real: 'That's really it. It is a kind of obsession: until they are out there, I am obsessed, in the good sense of the word.' Her style involves reinterpreting reality, creating sugar-coated versions of the things that interest her, in a medium that offers her an infinite range of possibilities. Using needles ranging from 3 to 25 mm, she sees her art as part of the knitting renaissance

that began a few years ago and which has generated the form of street art known as yarn bombing, a movement that breaks all the rules and shakes up the old-fashioned image of knitting: 'I love the idea of promoting an ancient craft associated with housewives and grandmothers. For me it is a kind of gentle protest.' In addition to commissions and personal projects, Emmanuelle also gives sewing and knitting lessons in Berlin, where she has lived since 2009, with a view to taking knitting the next level, whatever that may be: 'I don't yet know how, but it probably involves working as a collective of some kind.'

LEIGH MARTIN

PLACE OF RESIDENCE
OKLAHOMA CITY, USA

PLACE OF BIRTH
BARTLESVILLE, OKLAHOMA, USA

DATE OF BIRTH **1983**

WEBSITE
LEIGHMARTINART.COM

Leigh Martin, a lover of nature, lives in the heart of Oklahoma. Her textile work, photographs and installations are strongly influenced by her background in urban forestry. During her career as an artist and forest ranger, she became more and more fascinated by ecology and natural processes and now wants to use her artistic practice to communicate her fascination with the small details of the natural world. Her art emphasizes the importance of connecting with nature and maintaining an awareness of our surroundings, which she feels is crucial to living a fulfilling and creative life.

As a certified arborist, she is fascinated by trees and forests. After learning the basics of knitting from her mother, she began to create knitted pieces, and it remains the medium with which she feels most at ease. She says her art is mainly self-taught but that the subject of her work is as important as the work itself and that she finds it satisfying to combine her two passions in a creative way.

Using mainly wool (dyed using non-chemical colours and chosen for its texture and its ability to hold a shape) but also incorporating natural materials such as pine needles or poplar seeds, Leigh draws

Above left:
Detail of *Asperula,*
from the *Missing
Pieces* series, 2016

Above:
False Turkey Tail, from
the *52 Forms of Fungi*
series, 2014

her inspiration from nature's minutiae, especially fungi, lichens and plants that grow in extreme conditions. She is hugely inspired by the way organisms within an ecosystem cooperate, and close observation of these details lies at the origin of all her works. She is also very interested in the intangible benefits of nature, benefits that she believes have both a mental and a social impact on us.

Aside from her knitted pieces themselves, one of the most striking aspects of her work is the natural settings in which she places her creations. Most of her works are site-specific and she immortalizes them in photographs before dismantling them.

She loves the contrast between wool and the natural subjects that she is representing, with the stitches giving her knitted fungi a delicate

Opposite:
Incarnata, from
the *Missing Pieces*
series, 2016

Below:
Velvet Foot Fungus, from the
52 Forms of Fungi series, 2014

Above:
Tubes, 2015

Above:
Indigo Milky Cap, from the
52 Forms of Fungi series, 2013

Overleaf:
*Decomposition:
Colony II*, 2012

surface that reflects their subtle textures and patterns. Inspired by the art of Andy Goldsworthy, which he integrates into urban or natural locations, she defines her work as 'environmental art' and wants her outdoor installations to encourage people to remain aware of the natural world around them. She says that she learns a lot from her research into different species, which includes looking at guidebooks, technical data and illustrations. This new knowledge gives her further inspiration and so the cycle continues.

The dyes she used are carefully selected from a broad palette and her stitches are carefully chosen. Once she has found the right wool (usually by touch) and the right tools (double-pointed 3 or 3.5 mm needles) she begins to knit in an improvised way, generally changing each piece as she goes along, ready for its installation, which is her stage of the process. Even though she often has to knit large numbers of small pieces that will then be assembled into a bigger work, shaped by internal wires, she find the process very meditative and moves fluidly from one stage to another as her idea gradually takes shape.

For the *Decomposition* series (overleaf), her first incursion into art and still one of her favourite works, she spent a year knitting a colony of tiny mushroom caps, which became her first installation in Oregon in summer 2012. She regards this as a key stage in her artistic career.

Another landmark in Leigh's art career came with her series *52 Forms of Fungi*, begun in 2013, which not only enabled her to broaden her concept of knitting but also became a useful creative exercise. She says that at the time she felt much more restricted in her creative thinking than she does now.

Given that wool tends to lose its shape with humidity and to discolour when left outdoors for a long time, she has now begun to use other yarns for projects that are designed to withstand the elements.

Above:
Picus Taeda
Piece knitted from pine needles, 2013

Opposite:
Contained Aesthetics, 2016
With the help of volunteers, Leigh Martin knitted a vine for two months in a basketball court in Oklahoma City; the image shows the knitting after 15 days.

PLACE OF RESIDENCE
LETHBRIDGE, CANADA

PLACE OF BIRTH
LETHBRIDGE, CANADA

DATE OF BIRTH **1980**

WEBSITE
SHANELLPAPP.COM

SHANELL PAPP

Above:
Figure in White
60 × 177 cm
Knitting, crochet, weaving, sewing, moulding, beads, mannequin, various yarns, plastic, polyurethane rubber, 2015–16

Opposite:
The Hunting Party
300 × 213 cm
Knitting, crochet, sewing, paint, moulding, beads, mannequin, various yarns, plastic, fabric, glass, hair, clay, paint, 2014–15

Shanell Papp lives in Canada, very close to the mountains, with her partner Jarrett and their cat Warlock. She has a degree from the University of Lethbridge and another from the University of Saskatchewan and teaches at the University of Lethbridge as well as working in the public library. She likes the idea of being part of an academic and research environment without being a student and loves to work without any outside influence or direction.

Fascinated by the history of art and medicine and the human body, she has a great interest in mummified bodies, cannibalism, horrible crimes, antisocial behaviour – in short, anything that crosses the boundaries of the socially acceptable. Although she is interested in people, she does not particularly like talking to them and her work is primarily derived from observation alone. She feels more at ease when she is 'invisible' and likes working in libraries so that she can consult books and study her fellow human beings, finding them wonderfully mysterious and endlessly absorbing.

At the age of ten, she learned the basics of weaving, knitting, crochet and embroidery from her grandmother who ran a junk store with a fabulous stock of various bits and pieces that she could use to experiment: it was the perfect place to pursue a free apprenticeship in textile art. As a student Shanell came to admire Louise Bourgeois, Kiki Smith and the work of the Young British Artists. Later on, she was attracted to the work of David Altmejd, Shary Boyle, Marcel Dzama and Geoffrey Farmer, while

today she is most inspired by pop-culture disciplines such as comic books and cartoons.

Shanell uses all kinds of yarn and oddments that she picks up in junk shops or that people give her, occasionally including more expensive yarn. She likes to bring different materials together in a collage-like way, but wool remains the yarn she knows best. It seemed self-evident for her to begin to work with textiles since the medium did not require any specific tools or training. Focusing on fear and her own sense of powerlessness, she creates humanoid monsters and tries to reflect their mindsets. She claims that the time required to create terrifying works based on horrific subjects, in both the research and the production phases, almost drives her crazy.

Shanell works at home or in a cellar that she's converted into a studio. People have been heard to claim that her cellar is haunted but she insists it isn't true. She doesn't believe in ghosts but likes the idea that people can sense supernatural forces and she believes it makes her studio more powerful, detached from the rest of the world. She likes testing out ideas away from indiscreet eyes, and never talks about what she is working on until it is finished, be it to partner, family or strangers; she's even willing to lie about her current project

Above:
Severed Head #3
60 × 122 cm
Crocheted yarn, 2016

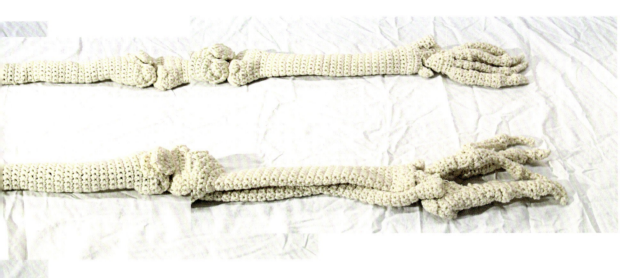

or hide it away if anyone insists on visiting her studio unexpectedly. She sees no point in critiquing a half-finished piece, as that is not helpful and her work is not intended to be collaborative.

While aware of the many advantages of working with textiles, she regrets that it's often seen as a feminine hobby and isn't granted the same respect as painting or sculpture. As she combines textiles with other crafts, she is interested in the way certain kinds of work are devalued, especially in North America where, in her view, manual skills are neither widespread nor widely recognized. Almost everything is mass-produced, with a very limited life span: people produce things as fast as possible, at the lowest cost, and then throw them away when they are broken.

Shanell also takes photographs and draws. Her works influence each another, with her textiles being reinterpretations of ideas she tackles in her photographs or drawings. She sees these activities as closely connected with her social environment and thinks she could have worked differently if she had grown up in a place where other materials were widely accessible. She also produces paintings, but never shows her painted work. In fact, she loves the idea that artists need to have a realm that they keep secret.

GISÈLE TOULOUZAN

PLACE OF RESIDENCE
**MONTREUIL AND
HYÈRES, FRANCE**

PLACE OF BIRTH
HYÈRES, FRANCE

DATE OF BIRTH **1950**

WEBSITE
GISELETOULOUZAN.COM

Member of the collective
Fiber Art Fever!

For Gisèle Toulouzan, art is predominantly playful and humour is always at the heart of her creative work. She borrows her subjects from famous paintings that she loves or from photographs she takes, capturing intimate moments between strangers. The joy of her art lies in using a technique she describes as 'ordinary, overlooked, undervalued' to recreate images such as the Mona Lisa in the guise of a 1950s housewife, seated serenely in front of her refrigerator (p. 197). The artist calls these 'my own small windows opened onto the cult of art history; my actions turn them into constructions of my own, creating both a synthesis of the past and a highly contemporary object.'

After she learned to knit at a young age thanks to her Italian grandmother, Gisèle's complex creative world was shaped by her studies at the School of Fine Arts in Aix-en-Provence, followed by

Above:
Nude
52 × 43 cm,
2015

Above:
Kiss
40 × 40 cm, 2014

Left:
Cigarette
16 × 4 cm, 2016

an MA in psychology, a degree in Italian and training as an art therapist. She has been a psychologist, a translator, an art therapist and the editor of a craft magazine, but throughout these many careers, she has never stopped painting, in oils or acrylics, and still regularly shows her work in galleries.

Inspired by the great Italian and Dutch masters, she began by reappropriating their works, distorting them and thus turning them

Below:
After Courbet
68 × 56 cm, 2016

Opposite:
Untitled
Height 40 cm, 2013

into a kind of tribute, while at the same time demystifying them. She chooses her subjects and models from museums, galleries and art books, with Duchamp, Manet and the American feminists remaining her favourites. Now the internet has opened up new pathways and suggests new subjects for her to explore, while still letting her give free rein to her wit. Her knitted art is a rejection of society's stereotypical and belittling attitude to what it views as 'women's work'. Knitting is just photography or painting by different means,

'My works are a bit like my children.'

After Massimo Vitali
129 × 63 cm, 2014

with the image no longer laid out on paper or canvas but becoming part and parcel of the material from which it is made: a long skein of coloured wool, knitted with two long needles. Her early works proved laborious to make: not liking the colours of the wool, which looked less delicate than those of paintings, she would touch them up with acrylic paint or coloured ink. Over time, she finally found a way of shading the colours and her stock of wools grew ever larger. Today she has a wide palette of colours to choose from and scarcely ever has to touch them up. Although it can take a long time to achieve the end result, sometimes more than a month, she loves the technique and is constantly surprised by what it can produce. In fact, the image does not emerge in full until the knitted work is completely finished and has been stretched.

She regards every piece as her best work at the time of making it and always feels a strong, almost maternal attachment to it. In the early days, and sometimes still today, she would immediately reknit a piece that had just been sold, terrified at the idea of being separated from it. Armed with her needles and using only woollen yarn, she knits easily, steadfastly and with a sense of humour, driven by an irrepressible desire to create: 'I cannot stop myself doing it. I think of nothing else, it is stronger than anything else.' When she is not busy with her art, she visits galleries and museums.

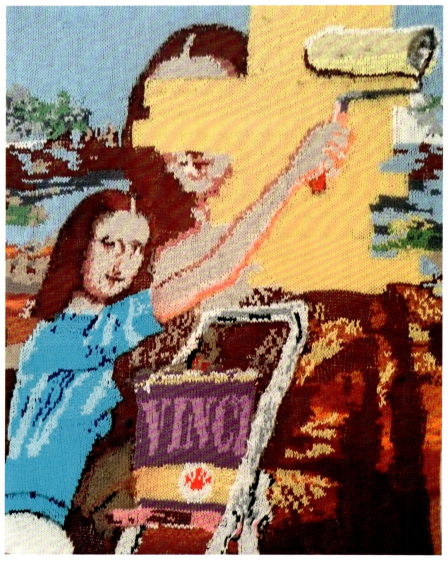

Almanarre Beach
75 × 50 cm, 2016

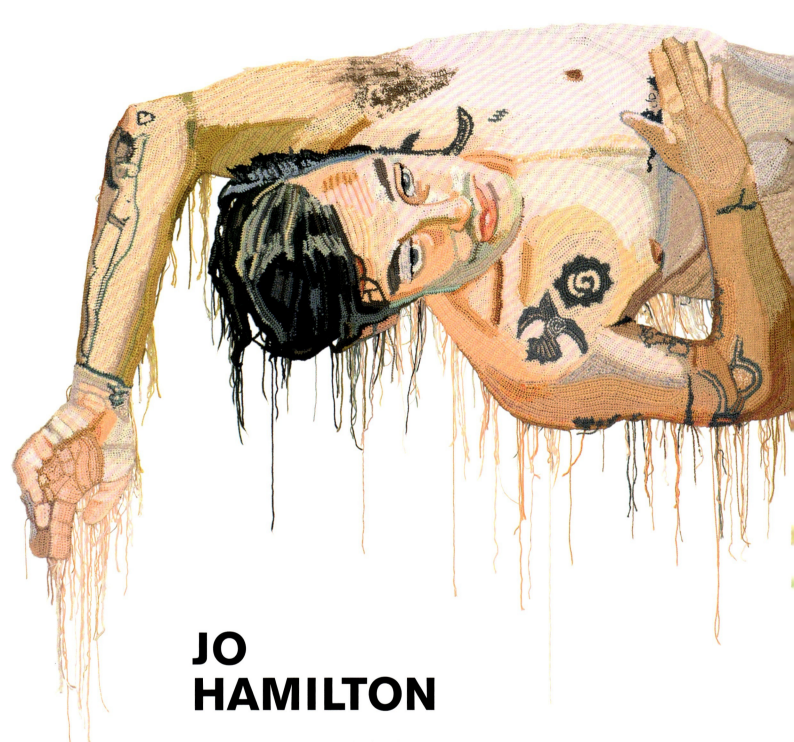

JO HAMILTON

PLACE OF RESIDENCE
**PORTLAND,
OREGON, USA**

PLACE OF BIRTH
GLASGOW, UK

DATE OF BIRTH **1972**

WEBSITE
JOHAMILTONART.COM

Jo Hamilton grew up in Scotland and in the 1990s she studied drawing and painting at Glasgow School of Art. After graduating, she moved to the United States. Her studio is a real haberdashery full of balls of yarn arranged by colour and shade. There, seated comfortably on her futon, she crochets portraits of celebrities, strangers she sees around her, residents at the local care centre for people living with

AIDS (where she does voluntary work), mysterious masked women, large-format male nudes, dogs and also cityscapes, like those of Portland, Oregon, where she now lives and works.

She crochets from photographs, with no preliminary research or sketches, observing, stitching and unpicking until the basic concept appears, picking out the colours and yarn she needs from her shelves: 'I can test out many different colours until I am satisfied.'

Growing up in a family that knitted and crocheted, she has always felt very close to the arts of needlework and other crafts. Her mother

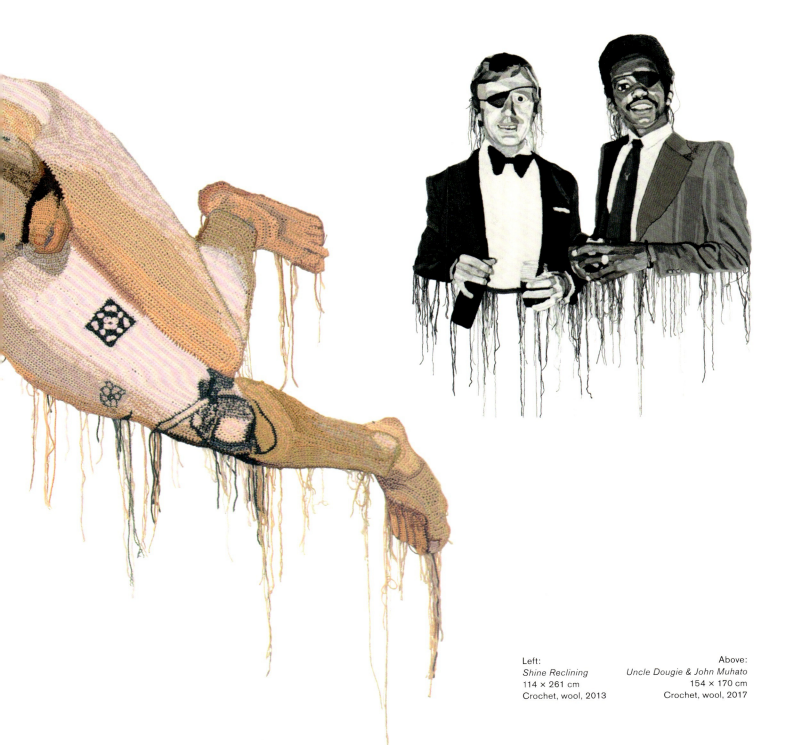

Left:
Shine Reclining
114 × 261 cm
Crochet, wool, 2013

Above:
Uncle Dougie & John Muhato
154 × 170 cm
Crochet, wool, 2017

and grandmother taught her knitting and crochet when she was six. She went back to knitting as a teenager and began to make presents for her friends, then gave it up again until 2006, the year when she exchanged her brush and tubes of paint for a crochet hook and a ball of yarn. The technique is now second nature and allows her to explore the genres and conventions of Western arts and crafts, while also offering her a means of reinventing and reinterpreting them.

When she began to work with a crochet hook, she felt she was really going back to basics. With that in mind she examined and revisited some of the genres of traditional art, including portraits, landscapes and nudes – with nudes revealing themselves a real challenge to her: 'I felt that if I could convincingly render a nude in crocheted yarn, I would prove to myself that I could really crochet anything.' In any case she is unable to resist the contradictions and humour inherent in the concept of producing a nude male figure made up entirely of soft and delicate knots: 'I've now completed two realistic-ish male nudes and dozens of portraits so I feel like my work may be heading towards abstraction.'

'I am concerned with how our preconception of artist, medium and subject combine to form the meaning and value of an art work and its subject.'

I Crochet Portland
160 × 189 cm
Crochet, wool, 2006−9

Passionate about colour, which she uses with both boldness and delicacy, she has a deep respect for all creative processes. She uses crochet to capture colour, light, time and expressions, in just the same way as she once did with painting and drawing. She regards crochet itself as having its own universal and ancient language, unchanged by the history of art, and sees it as an alternative to painting, existing independently of the fine arts but allowing itself to be used in a similar way to discuss ideas, ask questions and carry meaning.

When creating a portrait, Jo always begins with the eyes, using the crochet rows like outlines to define the structure of the face and working from the centre outwards until she has captured her subject in stitches. As the individual stitches join up to form a whole, she sees them as designating units of time and revealing the physical process behind the work.

By reviving a traditional technique, Jo Hamilton creates figurative pieces that tackle the issues of representation in society and in art, and rehabilitates the contemporary image of the crafts. Problems connected with social status and progress – like those that disfigure the town where she lives – and the question of what is represented or ignored are central to her work. Passionately concerned with the inversion of male and female roles and the question of identity in contemporary art and society, she tries to overturn sexist stereotypes.

Groucho Gia
129 × 91 cm
Crochet,
wool, 2013

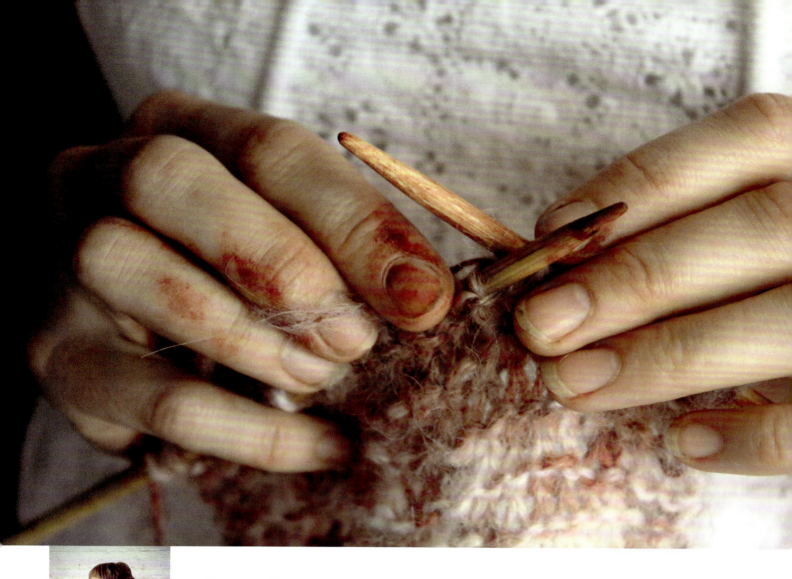

CASEY JENKINS

PLACE OF RESIDENCE
MELBOURNE, AUSTRALIA

PLACE OF BIRTH
MELBOURNE, AUSTRALIA

DATE OF BIRTH **1979**

WEBSITE
CASEY-JENKINS.COM

Casey Jenkins's installations and performances explore notions of intimacy and identity and the interplay of modes of power, whether individual or institutional, perceived or concrete. Her work ranges from meditative to disruptive and engages audiences around the world as she redefines structures of power and influence through street art, experimental performance and the destabilization of the notions of ownership and authorship of art. She rallies other artists and the public to collaborate with her on her creations and regards herself as a feminist performance artist. As a militant and feminist, she wants to pay tribute to women and appropriate the craft techniques traditionally associated with them, such as knitting and crochet. Working with the Craft Cartel group which was set up in 2007 as part of the 'craftivism' movement, she gets involved with street art projects and collaborative protest works, while also creating her own performance pieces and installations. All she says about her past is that she has a phobia of institutions and has never managed to stay in one for long, whether during her studies or in her professional life. She even declares she has learned absolutely everything from the internet and the generosity of her friends, saying that YouTube and WikiHow are her real teachers.

Above and opposite:
Casting Off My Womb
Performance over a period of 28 days (complete menstrual cycle), 2013
Finished length 16 m
Darwin Visual Arts Association (DVAA), Australia

'My favourite technique, for the process rather than the result, is finger knitting because it feels carnal.'

Above and right:
*Give Us a Smile, Sweetheart
(Dyke, Whore, Slut)*
150 × 180 cm
Baby's blanket knitted in silk
and UV-sensitive wool, 2016

Opposite:
Programmed to Reproduce
70 × 50 cm
Performance over a period of
7 days and 35 hours, 2016
Festival of Live Art,
Melbourne, Australia
Casey received several
thousand abusive online
comments following her
work *Casting Off My Womb*,
and recreated some of the
comments using yarn stained
with menstrual blood.

Fascinated by those who fight tirelessly for justice and equality, she has a deep admiration for the countless women and transgender people who have devoted all their energy to the arts or crafts, but whose names have sadly been lost in history. She believes the sum of their courage, energy and fight for survival has built a space from which present and future generations can draw strength.

In 2007 she began to depict women's genitalia in her series *Cunt Fling-Ups*, throwing them up on structures and power-lines much in the way gangs mark their territory by flinging shoes. She says she flung them alone or with groups of women and trans people and that, as feminists, they all saw this as a way to regain territory. She likes the robustness, persistence and practicality of yarn and deplores the fact that knitting is not regarded as a legitimate art form capable of representing complex concepts. For her, yarn evokes images associated with femininity and delicacy. Although she finds that it takes time to create a piece with wool, she admits that knitting offers her a broad range of sculptural possibilities. The processes of knitting and the manual arts, which are rhythmic and innately reliant on the movements of the body, lend themselves particularly well to the playfulness of artistic performances.

Casey wants to represent herself as honestly as possible in her work, no matter how that work is perceived, and is firmly resolved to express opinions that may at times seem disturbing. A fervent activist, she tries to rally people to her cause with wit and humour, always seeking to make her work accessible to all. Adapting her artistic approach to suit what she wants to express, she begins by considering the best means of representing her idea, preferring to learn the technique it requires rather than creating works that derive from a specific process, as when she decided to hack the digital systems of an obsolete knitting machine from the 1990s.

Below and right:
sMother
Performance over a
period of a week, 2016
Venice International
Performance Art Week, Italy

Casey is currently working around the issue of hidden genders and on the history of women and trans people, whose voices have deliberately been stifled and ignored. To condemn attempts to prevent society from expressing itself, she created a 'blanket of shame' (p. 208) for the Melbourne Midsummer Festival. This baby's blanket, embroidered with the words 'Give us a smile, sweetheart', conceals another message that is invisible to the naked eye: the words 'dyke', 'whore' and 'slut' are knitted in UV-sensitive yarn, becoming visible only when the blanket is exposed to sunlight. Along the same lines, Casey performed a work named *Programmed to Reproduce* (p. 209), using yarn partly stained with menstrual blood to machine-knit copies of some of the abusive comments she's received online.

AURÉLIE
MATHIGOT

PLACE OF RESIDENCE
PARIS, FRANCE

PLACE OF BIRTH
PARIS, FRANCE

DATE OF BIRTH **1974**

WEBSITE
AURELIEMATHIGOT.COM

Trained in art history and philosophy at the Sorbonne, Paris, and a graduate of the École des Beaux Arts in Aix-en-Provence, Aurélie Mathigot has revived the art of the needle for the contemporary world, using embroidery, knitting and crochet. After pondering which medium she should choose to make three-dimensional works, she discovered the universal language of textiles, especially crochet, which she has been pursuing for a dozen or so years. A photographer, sculptor and embroiderer, she now creates sculptures using wool, cotton and rope. The crochet stitches cover or line found objects and pieces of furniture taken from her everyday life. Using the illusion of reality as her leitmotif, she creates a parallel universe by wrapping pieces of furniture, pianos, knick-knacks, tools, cutlery and other objects in order to change their appearance. The crocheted covers envelop the items like a second skin and reflect their complexity, making us question our relationship with objects in a humorous and poetic manner. Exacting and always on the alert, Aurélie is constantly using her crochet hook to ask questions about life and art , sometimes combining her works with photography, video, wax or ceramics. She says she is following in the footsteps of Louise Bourgeois and Joseph Beuys and is fascinated by the complex artistic worlds of Richard Deacon, Chopin, Walter Benjamin, Comme des Garçons, Camille Corot, Michaël Borremans, Sophie Taeuber-Arp, Peter Doig and Wim Vandekeybus. She is interested in the concept of obsolescence, creates optical illusions and captures the passage of

Above left:
My Father, The Hero
Tools covered in crochet,
cotton, silk, linen, 2007

Above right:
*I Will Never Be
Able To Marry, I've
Covered The Cutlery*
Cutlery covered in crochet,
cotton, silk, linen, 2007

Above left:
Vanitas
290 × 95 cm
Crochet, organic cotton,
carved wood, plaited
straw, mirror, 2008

Above right:
*Fuck the Aperitif, I Have
No Friends Tonight*
Metal cup, crochet, raw linen
yarn, silver chain, 2012

time through her works in large and small formats, seeing the crochet hook as a rudimentary tool that suggests both elongation and extension. Steeped in contemporary art, she is interested in difficult issues and in the 'anxieties that keep you awake at night', using her work to explore the notions of unrealistic idealism and of love: 'I laugh a lot so as not to die of suffocation.'

These questions are the motivating force behind her creative process. Her approach consists of observing and experimenting with everyday life, while mixing different media, as in the case of *Hunter's Dinner* (opposite), made of wood, ceramic, plaster, wax and crocheted linen, rope, wool and cotton. She crochets and embroiders in her studio, on the train or wherever she happens to be, and alongside the women she meets in France or during her trips abroad, to Mexico, Brazil and also India. She is not afraid of big challenges, such as *Vanitas* (p. 213), a crochet sculpture made up of 900 pieces of wooden fruit covered in unbleached cotton, or *Into the Wild* (right) with its 150,000 wooden lollipop sticks sewn onto Mexican hemp bags, surrounded by crocheted fringes in wool, linen, silk, rope and cotton. Keen to pass on her techniques, she has designed works in collaboration with other artisans who want to share their expertise, including the lace-makers of Calais and others who preserve the textile art traditions of their own countries, especially India, Mexico and Brazil.

For Aurélie, the yarn, the stitches, the maker and their skill all come together give shape to a knitted work, like a protective membrane that envelops everything and gives strength both to the objects and to their maker.

Aurélie Mathigot was awarded the City of Paris Design Prize in the 'crafts' category in 2011.

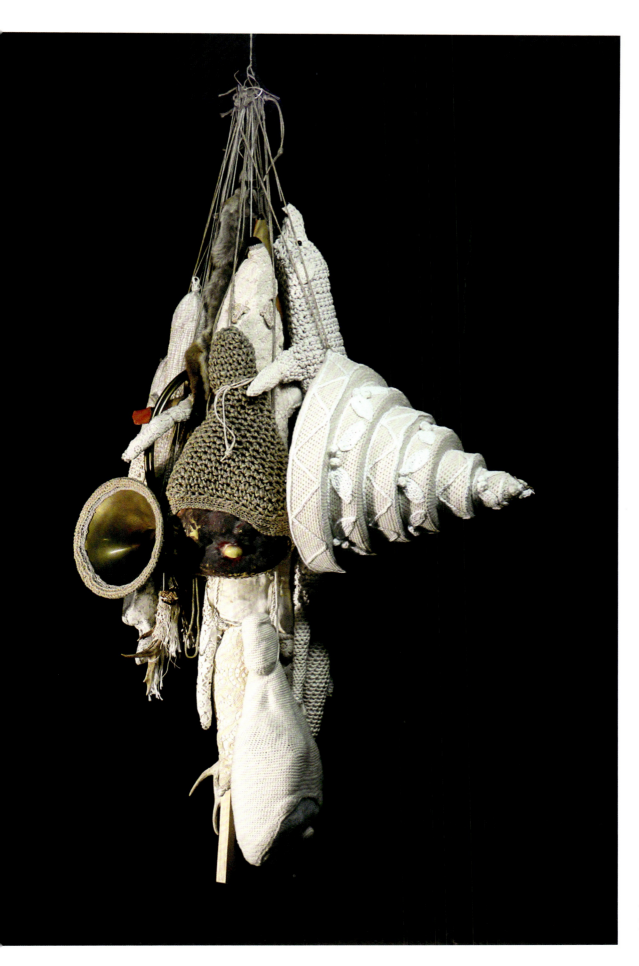

Left:
Hunter's Dinner
310 × 140 cm
Mixed media: ceramic,
wood, plaster, wax,
crocheted linen rope,
wool, cotton and
silk, 2012

NOORTJE DE KEIJZER

PLACE OF RESIDENCE
UTRECHT, NETHERLANDS

PLACE OF BIRTH
ROOSENDAAL, NETHERLANDS

DATE OF BIRTH **1987**

WEBSITE
NOORTJEDEKEIJZER.COM

Noortje de Keijzer grew up in the Netherlands in a small and charmless industrial town, which was originally a tiny village then rapidly grew when it became the site of a factory.

She remembers her childhood as a reassuring and quite restricted environment, in which she was pushed to be as creative and imaginative as she wanted to be. Loving interior decoration and design products, she enrolled in an art school, the Design Academy of Eindhoven, which had a very good international reputation at the time. There she worked with a variety of different materials, specializing in textile design. Today she creates as a way of dealing with the complexity of life, putting her problems in perspective and finding solutions.

She regards Frank Visser, from Studio IJM, as a kind of mentor, particularly loving the way he uses colour to create atmosphere and his ability to tell stories using design and photography. She is also inspired by all determined, authentic and passionate people who devote their life to what they do best, in whatever field.

She began to be interested in knitting during her studies but does not consider herself a good technician, preferring to ask faster, more skilled knitters to execute the work for her. She collaborates with a specialist in industrial knitting in the Netherlands, who puts her templates into a knitting machine and advises her on which yarns to use. As a designer, she believes it is only the result that counts. She therefore surrounds herself with professionals who can help her translate her ideas as accurately as possible.

For each of her projects, Noortje chooses the materials and techniques most likely to suit the atmosphere she wants to create and the story she wants to tell. She likes wool because it looks natural and is

Above left and right:
My Knitted Boyfriend
Knitted in 10% alpaca, 50% merino, 40% acrylic yarn, 2011

timeless. She is most strongly drawn to the technique of knitting, seeing it as a very graphic and structured process, in which every stitch is like a pixel; she likes the repetitive network formed by knitted stitches, which looks simple and minimalist but can also be highly architectural, and also the tactile stimulus that knitting involves. She believes that knitted objects evoke a sense of warmth, comfort, security and nostalgia.

Knitting has been part of her life for as long as she can remember. Her grandmother knitted extensively, both by hand and machine, captivating the young Noortje as she turned woollen yarn into objects. The advantages of the technique are the naturalness of wool, the sense of warmth and softness it produces, as well as its resistance to water and dirt. Nevertheless, Noortje notes that like all techniques, knitting has its limits. She does not enjoy its 'mathematical' aspects and the counting that it involves. As a perfectionist, she wants everything to look flawless and is jubilant when the pieces of her work finally come together.

Lemon Cushion (p. 219) is both a lemon and a cushion: 'Because when life gives you lemons, we all need a soft knitted bright yellow lemon on our couch to hide behind, don't we?' The cushion is accompanied by a small risograph print designed by the graphic studio We Are Out Of Office, based in Utrecht. The idea is that the cushion will brighten up the home and bring the sunshine indoors, even when it is raining outside.

'I like to show a cheerful reflection of the world around us and I hope to bring positivity to the world.'

My Knitted Boyfriend, a graduation project she began towards the end of her studies in 2011, brings together her love of storytelling, fashion and product design. Five years on, it remains very topical and speaks to many people who, rather than just saying they like it or don't like it, tend to have strong opinions and emotions about it. She believes that this work has no limits and in a sense exists at a distance from the times and society in which we live. *My Knitted Boyfriend* is a pillow with a personality, a cushion to cuddle and caress: 'This man is always happy. He likes to sit on your floor, on your couch or at your dinner table. But most of all he likes to lay down next to you in bed.' At the moment there are two variant designs: light-skinned Arthur and dark-skinned Steve.

'Loneliness is an important subject in the time we're living in,' she explains. 'We are searching for the romantic idea of "the right one" in our lives. With very high expectations!' She came up with the idea because so many people find it difficult, if not impossible, to find the partner of their dreams and many live alone (regardless of age, sex, culture or language), dreaming of someone to cuddle and sit beside on the sofa – for it is the ordinary moments when people can feel most lonely: 'With this man, you can be sure he will never leave you!' *My Knitted Boyfriend* is a humorous project about a serious subject; she believes that 'laughing about a negative feeling is already the beginning of a more positive and happy feeling. And when you feel positive and happy with yourself, loneliness will disappear!'

Above:
My Knitted Boyfriend
Knitted in 10% alpaca, 50%
merino, 40% acrylic yarn, 2011

Opposite:
Lemon Cushion
Knitted in 50% viscose,
50% acrylic yarn, 2016

DOMINIQUE KAEHLER SCHWEIZER

PSEUDONYM
MADAME TRICOT

PLACE OF RESIDENCE
**WIL/SAINT-GALL,
SWITZERLAND**

PLACE OF BIRTH
**BELLEVILLE-SUR-LOIRE,
FRANCE**

DATE OF BIRTH **1948**

WEBSITES
MADAMETRICOT.CH AND
**TRICOTGOURMAND.
BLOGSPOT.COM**

Dominique Kaehler Schweizer, alias Madame Tricot, has spent all her life trying to push at boundaries without breaking them, preferring to stretch them in order to go even further. Following her inner voice and not caring what anyone else says, she is passionately and profoundly involved in whatever interests her. That led her to leave France at the age of twenty-six in order to marry a Swiss German and set up home near Lake Constance where she has been working for forty years as a doctor, psychiatrist and naturopath. Later, with her second husband, she began to breed medicinal leeches and to write scientific works on leech therapy, while her life as an artist remained on the back burner until her retirement in 2012.

In December of that year, when she was only knitting scarves and hats, she had a flash of inspiration while watching a cookery show on

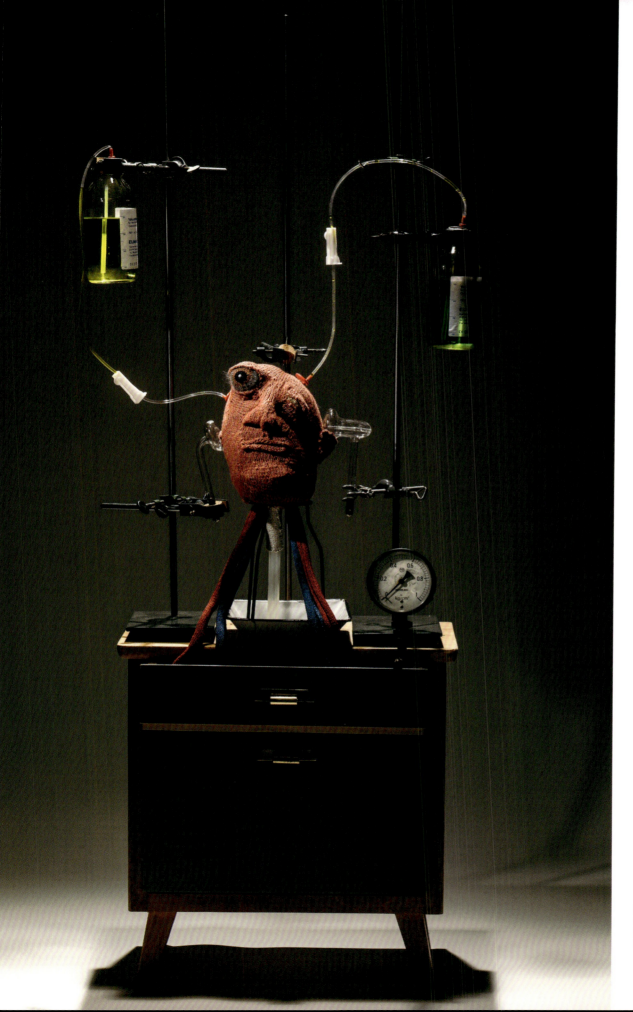

Left:
Dr Kaehler Schweizer's Laboratory of Applied Genetics, 2014

Opposite:
Cheeses, 2013–15

Left:
*Canapés:
Mini-Pizzas*, 2015

television in which a chef was preparing fish. She immediately began to knit a sea bream. Surprised at how realistic the result looked, she decided to continue this adventure by knitting another bream, but this time carved up, with its head cut off and the bones visible. It was followed by a remarkably detailed Bresse chicken. In May 2012 a wool seller in Winterthur asked her to recreate a butcher's counter in her shop. That encounter marked a turning point in her success and the media and museums now began to show an interest in her remarkably realistic woollen pig's heads. Dominique has been invited to New York by *Vogue* magazine and was awarded the St Gallen Culture Prize in 2015. In 2016, the American journal *Fiber Art Now* named her 'emerging textile artist' of the year.

As a result of her medical training, she is fascinated by life, death and the rapid passage of time. She has a preference for the absurd and for dark humour and likes to be provocative, unlike traditional knitters who, she believes, are not always aware of the fact that you can use a ball of wool and a needle to make something other than socks. She declares loudly and openly that she is an artist and wants to combat the prejudices surrounding knitting, which she regards as a means of expression that is just as valid as any other, saying that 'painters also use textiles, especially canvas, for their paintings.'

Inspired by food and anatomy in general, she has been linked with Eat Art, a movement that appeared in the 1960s under the influence of the Swiss artist Daniel Spoerri. She particularly loves the work of Max Bottini and Claes Oldenburg (known for his monumental installations and replicas of ordinary objects) and greatly admires, among others, Jean Tinguely, Louise Bourgeois and Vivienne Westwood. Her dream would be to create a monumental metal and knitted work in collaboration with Jeff Koons.

Claiming to have no mentor, except perhaps her grandmother without whom she would never have learned the basics of knitting, she follows her intuition and says that she simply has a gift for crocheting and knitting in three dimensions. With no patterns or calculations, working purely from the images in her mind that want to be made real, she sets to work with the feeling that something within her is knitting without any conscious control, leading her towards a

Above, from left to right:
*Reliquaries:
God's Eye Is Watching You!;
Einstein's Brain (18 Months);
Immaculate Conception,
Or Why Storks Bring
Babies,* 2014–16

goal without her ever really knowing how she managed to get there, whether she's creating a head, a bodily organ or a piece of fruit: 'It always works: I never have to undo a work once I have begun it.'

She has always had a special relationship with textiles thanks to her mother who designed and collected fabrics, and loves wool because it is soft, pleasing to touch and lightweight, with a definite preference for cashmere and silk, as well as yak and camel hair. She is attracted to knitting because it is practical, sociable, repetitive and rhythmic, forcing the two hemispheres of the brain to stay connected and to keep intrusive thoughts at bay.

FREDDIE ROBINS

PLACE OF RESIDENCE
FEERING, UK

PLACE OF BIRTH
HITCHIN, UK

DATE OF BIRTH **1965**

WEBSITE
FREDDIEROBINS.COM

Freddie Robins teaches textiles at the Royal College of Art (RCA) in London. After taking a foundation course in art and design at Hastings, then studying knitted textiles at Middlesex Polytechnic and again at the RCA, she decided to specialize in this field. Trained as a fashion designer and with a particular liking for the art and techniques of knitting, the artist places her work firmly within the sphere of contemporary art.

When she speaks of her influences, she mentions in particular her godmother Pamela Darking, who taught her the technique of knitting, the fashion designer Patricia Roberts, and also *Wild Knitting*, a handbook of nonconformist knitting published in the early 1980s. As a student, she was inspired by the surrealist fashion designer Elsa Schiaparelli and by Zandra Rhodes's designs, as well as by the Scottish painter Alan Davie. She is also devoted to the work of the Japanese designers whose work is becoming increasingly popular in the West, such as Yohji Yamamoto and Comme des Garçons, not

Left:
Knitted Homes Of Crime
Hand-knitted wool, stuffing
Pieces knitted for the artist
by Jean Arkell, 2002

to mention the French designer Jean-Paul Gaultier, whom she was lucky enough to meet during one of her study projects. Nowadays, although she draws her inspiration from a number of artists including Paul Auster, Annette Messager, Sophie Calle, Louise Bourgeois and Frida Kahlo, she insists that she does not belong to any movement and has no mentor.

For the past twenty years she has been using wool as her artistic medium, regarding it as charged with cultural associations and therefore easy to subvert. She regards knitting as a 'non-aggressive technique', with which people feel at ease, but also a powerful tool when it is used to express complex or emotional issues.

Preferring to machine knit rather than by working by hand, she is motivated by a need and a deep desire to 'make', feeling reassured by objects that exist materially but have no material value in real terms,

Above:
Craft Kills
200 × 68 × 38 cm
Machine knitting,
hand knitting, 2002

Right and opposite,
below left:
*Skin, A Good
Thing To Live In*
201 × 190 cm
Machine knitting, 2002

and by the act of making them. Her work is a means of exploring, expressing, confronting and examining her emotions, without serving as therapy. She works alone in her studio, far from the busy Stitch'n Bitch clubs and yarn bombers, and spends all her time knitting what she calls 'inherently useless things'. Her knitting practice 'questions conformity and notions of normality' and she uses it as a medium for interpreting and coming to terms with the world she lives in. She uses the medium to explore contemporary issues relating to domesticity, gender and the human condition: 'My work subverts these preconceptions and disrupts the notion of the medium being passive and benign.'

Knitted Homes of Crime (pp. 228–29), which she describes as her most successful work, in terms of both technique and concept, is made up of seven hand-knitted tea-cosies in the shape of houses. They look sweet and benign but are in fact reproductions of the homes of female killers or the locations where they committed their

crimes: 'When someone commits a heinous crime, such as murder, they are damned, and when a woman commits it she is doubly damned, once for committing the crime and once for going against her sex.' Starting out from the postulate that women are widely expected to produce life and provide care, for this work Freddie chose murderesses who acted alone, without the involvement of a man. Her

Left:
I'm So Bloody Sad
98 × 40 × 210 cm
Machine knitting, foam,
sand, hand knitting,
2007–15

Below:
The Perfect – Alex
58 × 92 cm
Hand-knitted wool and
acrylic yarn, 2007

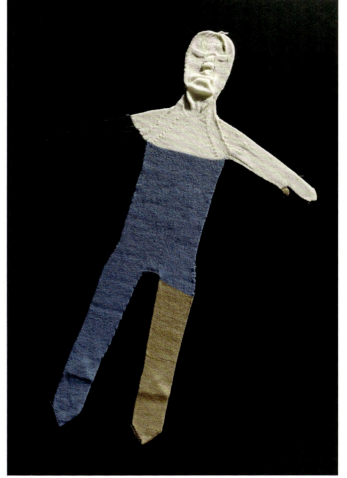

231

Right:
Untitled
13 × 21 × 5 cm
Machine knitting and
mixed media, 2013

Above:
One Letter Apart
170 × 55 × 43 cm
Machine and hand knitting,
crochet and mixed media
on oak base, 2013

knitted houses, inspired by her large collection of motifs as well as old and contemporary knitted objects, especially knitted tea-cosies in the form of picturesque country cottages, are faithful reproductions of these houses haunted by past crimes. In order to create each pattern, the artist used photos unearthed in books for some, while for others she went on location to photograph them herself. The *Knitted Homes of Crime* slowly took shape with the help of Jean Arkell, 'a very skilled and fast knitter' who created the bodies of the houses, onto which Freddie Robins then embroidered the tiny details. Over a period of seven months the two women exchanged yarns, patterns and crime stories by post.

Opposite, below:
Someone Else's Dream
Series of recycled
handmade sweaters,
mixed yarns, 2014–16

Right:
Limb
14 × 20 × 64 cm
Machine and hand knitting,
crochet and mixed media, 2013

ASHLEY V. BLALOCK

PLACE OF RESIDENCE
SAN DIEGO, USA

PLACE OF BIRTH
SAN DIEGO, USA

DATE OF BIRTH **1978**

WEBSITE
ASHLEYVBLALOCK.COM

An artist and art historian, Ashley V. Blalock works with crochet, which she sees as a meditative process in which every stitch is evidence of the work of her hands, allowing her to merge the arts and crafts. She creates objects and site-specific installations inspired by everyday artefacts from the domestic sphere and also by the Victorian period and Baroque art. Throughout her work, she explores the subject of discomfort and the coping mechanisms used to provide solace from the stress and trauma of modern life.

Ashley grew up in California where she earned a degree in painting and printmaking at the University of San Diego in 2000, an MA in art history at the University of California in 2005 and an MFA in sculpture at the San Francisco Art Institute in 2012.

Influenced by Caravaggio as well as by Christo and Jeanne-Claude, her art is driven by impulse. She works every day, without exception, and says she has so many ideas in her head that she cannot turn them into reality fast enough.

When she was six years old, her grandmother taught her the basic chain stitch used in crochet, and her great aunt showed her how to cast on. She then learned other crochet and knitting stitches from books.

Before she began to incorporate knitting into her work, Ashley used crochet only for personal projects, devoting herself almost

Above:
Complements (detail)
Variable dimensions
Crochet, extruded silicon,
embroidery thread, 2010

Opposite:
Keeping Up Appearances
365 × 760 × 365 cm
Crocheted cotton yarn, 2015
Installed at the exhibition
Processing Fiber at
250 Monroe, Grand
Rapids, Michigan

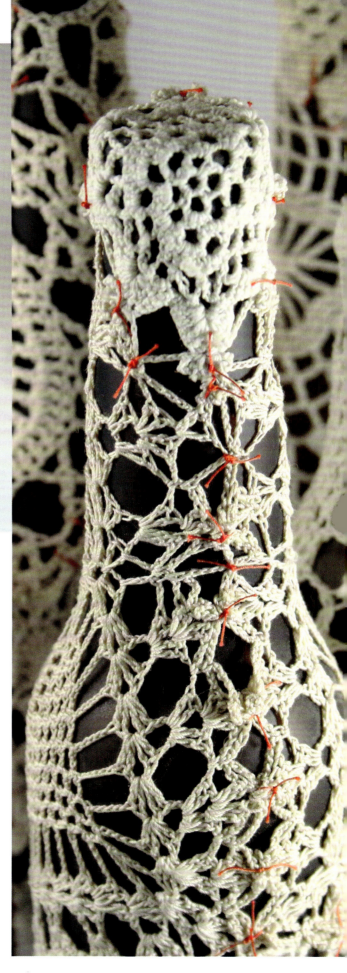

Above and right:
Six-Pack Comfort
25.5 × 20.5 × 20.5 cm
Crochet, beer bottles,
doilies, red yarn, 2010

entirely to oil painting, a technique she abandoned one evening when her dog rubbed its nose against the canvas and smudged the fresh paint.

The delicacy of her work means she has to use a very thin, strong yarn, usually red, white or black, which she crochets with steel hooks (between 0.75 and 11.5 mm). She rarely uses wool, finding it too fluffy for her extremely delicate works, but she does use it for creating personal objects, although she generally finds it too hot to wear in southern California, and has since been learning to spin it.

Keeping Up Appearances (p. 235), a work whose title is inspired by the BBC TV sitcom of the 1990s, consists of a row of giant crocheted doilies. Sculptures that are the same time monumental, complex and delicate, these doilies span what seem like dizzying heights, covering both the floor and the walls with bold red cotton yarn. Ashley's installations question the way individuals try to keep up appearances, at whatever cost. With their immoderate size, abstract and kaleidoscopic forms and intense colour, these doilies lose in delicacy what

Above and left:
Any Nine Months
360 × 7.5 cm
Crochet, cotton yarn,
contraceptive pill cases,
2013–present

they gain in strength. They captivate viewers and suggest that sometimes everyday things like lace doilies may cover up truths, ugliness and unpleasantness. Shown in 2016 at the Whatcom Museum in Bellingham, WA, in an exhibition entitled *Colorfast,* this installation, which took four days to set up, remains her most majestic work and she says she is very proud of it. Far removed from the lace doilies around the house by earlier generations to embellish or protect the surfaces of furniture or hide wear and tear, Ashley's doilies glow with bold colour and evoke a range of complex and at times menacing imagery, recalling of the symbolism of the white sheets used to cover the furniture in closed and abandoned houses.

'My work is either huge or tiny.
I don't seem to do anything in between.'

Below left:
*Feminist Fan #14 (Frida Kahlo
Self-Portrait: 1940)*
45 × 30 cm, 2015

Below right
*Feminist Fan #27 (A Portrait of the Artist
Orlan by Fabrice Lévêque in 1997)*
50 × 38 cm, 2016

KATE JUST

PLACE OF RESIDENCE
ST KILDA, AUSTRALIA

PLACE OF BIRTH
**HARTFORD,
CONNECTICUT, USA**

DATE OF BIRTH **1974**

WEBSITE
KATEJUST.COM

Kate Just sees herself first and foremost as a feminist artist. She lectures at the Victorian College of the Arts in Melbourne, Australia, and lives in the suburb of St Kilda, on the outskirts of Melbourne, with her daughter and her partner Paula.

She studied film making at Boston University, gained a PhD in sculpture at Monash University, then moved to Australia in the early 1990s, where she obtained a degree in fine arts at the Victorian College of the Arts. Although she has worked with a wide variety of techniques, in particular textiles, ceramics, collage and photography, she has been focusing on knitting for the past fifteen years. In 2000, following the tragic and brutal death of her brother, her mother taught her to knit. She believes that was the moment she realised that knitting could be a powerful tool, personally and politically and in poetic and narrative terms.

Since 2002 she has been creating works based around feminist representations of the body, using a range of media including resin, ceramics, collage, photography, textiles, and in particular knitting. Her knitted

Opposite:
*Feminist Fan #25 (Ana
Mendieta, Untitled
Facial Hair Transplant,
Moustache, 1972)*
45 × 30 cm
Hand knitting and
embroidery, 2016

Previous pages, left:
*Feminist Fan #15
(Claude Cahun,
Self-Portrait, 1927)*
Hand knitting and
embroidery, 2015

Previous pages, right:
*Feminist Fan #28 (Eva
Hesse photographed by
Hermann Landshoff)*
45 × 35 cm
Hand knitting and
embroidery, 2016

art works are invariably autobiographical and her earliest knit sculptures included a life-size statue of her father dressed in his police uniform (*Uniform/Dad*; p. 245), a family tree, based around her memories of climbing trees with her brother and sister (*Family Tree*), and a giant woollen hedge in the shape of the word 'LOVE', inspired by the Christmas decorations seen in suburban gardens on a drive through Connecticut (*Boundary*; p. 244). Her intensive work over the course of that year really allowed her to delve into her childhood experiences and family memories.

Kate then concentrated on ways of representing the female body and reinterpreted a number of legendary works by women artists, reflecting her own traumatic experiences, her sexual awakening and her desire to become a mother. She spent many years working on a series of knitted skins and suits of armour, exploring the suggestive and connective nature of skin and its ability to embody the concepts of femininity and subjectivity. In 2011 she started on a socially engaged series, *Knit Hope, Knit Safe* and *The Furies*, for which she invited women's representatives to knit public banners and take photographs condemning violence against women.

Her most recent work, *Feminist Fan*, is a series of hand-knitted homages to women artists of the world, including Sarah Lucas, Pussy

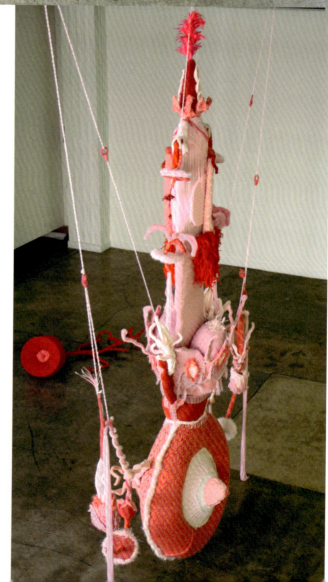

Opposite, above:
Red Fur Baby (piece from
The Garden of Interior Delights)
38 × 10 × 38 cm, 2008

Below:
The Arms of Mother
92 × 32 × 2 cm
Hand-knitted piece, 2012
City of Port Phillip collection

Opposite, below:
The Garden of Interior Delights
380 × 120 × 60 cm
Hand and machine knitting, plastic,
cardboard, ribbon, cable, stuffing,
wood, macramé rope, iron rings,
hooks, found objects, fur, 2008
City of Port Phillip collection

Right:
Postscript: A Burial Suit
218 × 89 × 69 cm, 2013
City of Port Phillip collection

Riot, the Guerrilla Girls, Cindy Sherman, Lynda Benglis, Juliana Huxtable, Mithu Sen, Tracey Moffatt, Yoko Ono, Hannah Wilke, Frida Kahlo (p. 242) and more. As autobiographical as the rest of her work, *Feminist Fan* is inspired by the way some groups of militant women, such as Femen and Pussy Riot, have managed to take over spaces, whether public or institutional, to condemn patriarchal institutions. The title of the work emphasizes her respect for these artists and the women's movement. A sign of true devotion to the cause, *Feminist Fan* is a work that proved extremely time-intensive, with each carefully knitted portrait requiring nearly 80 hours and more than 10,000 stitches to complete. This project has grown substantially over time and has now become a genuine feminist performance in which the body, textiles and all forms of adornment are used to question stereotypes about gender, sexuality and identity.

Based in an old knitwear factory converted into a studio, Kate combines painting and drawing with embroidery and knitting, working tirelessly and experimenting constantly to feed her creative process. She deplores the fact that textile techniques are

Left, above and below:
Fertile Ground
218 × 177 × 177 cm
Hand and machine
knitting, cardboard,
glue, papier mâché,
glass fibre, yarn,
adhesive tape,
glue, 2003

Below and bottom:
Uniform/Dad
Life size
Hand knitting, papier mâché,
wood, glass fibre, adhesive
tape, glue, 2002

time-consuming and that they are not regarded as having the same value as painting or sculpture on the traditional art market. Instead, however, she uses social networks such as Instagram (@katejustknits) to exhibit her works, further the feminist discourse and promote the technique of knitting as a genuine artistic medium. As a series, she regards *Feminist Fan* as an intimate portrait of feminism and her own influences, 'in which threads of connection between artists and across time and cultures emerge.'

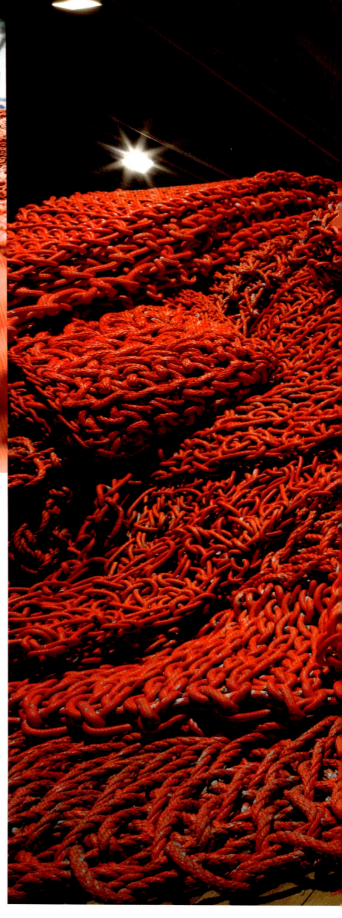

ORLY
GENGER

PLACE OF RESIDENCE
NEW YORK, USA

PLACE OF BIRTH
NEW YORK, USA

DATE OF BIRTH **1979**

WEBSITE
ORLYGENGER.COM

Orly Genger weaves webs and walls and covers entire rooms with rope. Her sprawling, monumental sculptures take over interior and exterior spaces and call on viewers to engage with them, inviting visitors to walk through them, touch them and absorb their bright colours. After graduating from Brown University in 2001, then the Art Institute of Chicago the following year, Orly became known for her large-scale installations.

Above left:
Terra
Recycled lobster
rope and paint, 2014
The Oklahoma Contemporary,
Oklahoma City

Right:
Big Boss
Recycled lobster rope
and paint, 2010
MASS MoCA, Massachusetts

While still a student, she began to use crochet, a technique she regarded at the time as a useful way to keep her hands busy. She only crochets by hand, saying that it never occurred to her to create anything, let alone to make sculptures, and that it just seemed to her that she needed to keep working. After spending months crocheting, she produced a number of pieces in various shapes and colours. That was the moment Orly decided to link them all together. Then something emerged, something with surprising physical strength and an underlying sense of motion that resembles the murmur of life, something that wanted to expand and develop and grow. For the first time, she saw crochet as a medium for sculpture, using the malleability of rope on both a small and a large scale.

Her fantastical crocheted landscape *Red, Yellow and Blue*, commissioned in 2011 by Madison Square Art, is surely the most majestic and powerful project she has ever undertaken. Weighing nearly 2 tonnes and covering a surface of about 1,400 square metres, the 400 kilometres of knotted and painted reclaimed lobster rope

Right:
Red, Yellow and Blue (detail)
Recycled lobster rope
and paint, 2013
Madison Square Park,
New York

Below:
Hurlyburly
Recycled lobster rope and paint, 2016
Waller Creek Conservancy,
Austin, Texas

Opposite, below right:
Puzzlejuice
Recycled lobster rope
and paint, 2016
Riverside Park, New York

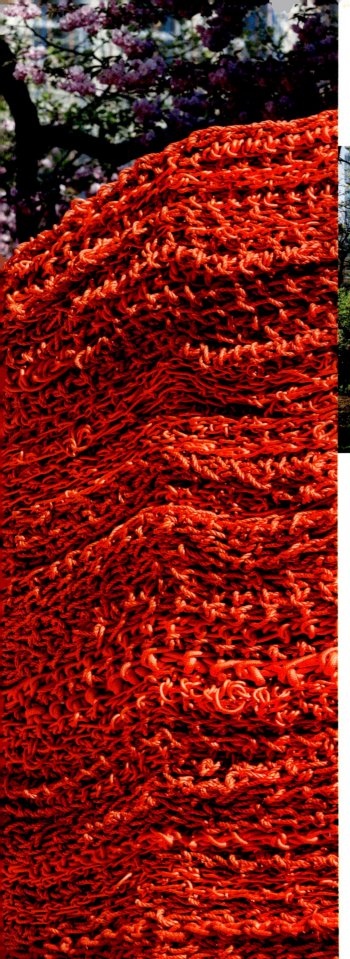

Left and below:
Red, Yellow and Blue (details)
Recycled lobster rope
and paint, 2013
Madison Square Park, New York

were unfurled across the grass of Madison Square Park, right in the middle of New York, turning the landscape red, yellow and blue. This project became central to her life for more than two years, occupying her mind constantly, as she feared she might run out of the material she needed: used rope she bought from fishermen who could no longer use it. Wet and covered in smelly fish scales, it weighed more than 45 tonnes when she acquired it. The previous life of the rope and its function were integral to the creative process of knotting it, a process that proved very trying, sometimes feeling like a struggle, sometimes like a synchronized dance. Physical challenges are a fundamental part of her work. *Red, Yellow and Blue* was inspired by a series of paintings entitled *Who's Afraid of Red, Yellow and Blue* by Barnett Newman, one of the major artists of the Abstract Expressionism movement and one of the first Color Field painters.

'I am fully engaged, both physically and intellectually.'

The installation *You*, also made from recycled lobster rope painted by hand, extended over a length of 70 metres on the Front Campus of Brown University. Creating meandering interruptions in landscapes both natural and planned, this iconic work undulates in a U-shape, creating a space that is both interactive and contemplative, drawing attention to the university's borders and embracing members of the Brown University community in its colourful woven arms. *You* was exhibited from November 2014 to June 2015.

By monumentalizing the practice of knotting and weaving, Orly takes this 'women's work' out of the domestic sphere. She draws on the formal language of large-scale sculptures by artists like Richard Serra and Donald Judd to create playful and inviting public installations. In her studio, photographs of Richard Serra, Frank Stella, Felix Gonzalez-Torres and Lynda Benglis are taped to the wall, alongside numerous pictures of bodybuilders, highlighting the physicality of her work. Since 2012, she has been working on smaller-scale aluminium and bronze pieces. Her cast-iron sculptures refer back to her iconic rope works as well as to her extremely detailed drawings and her many collages made up of comic-book superhero imagery.

Above, left and right:
Current
Recycled lobster rope
and paint, 2014
Contemporary Austin,
Austin, Texas

PICTURE CREDITS

ABOUT THE AUTHOR

Charlotte Vannier is a writer, photo stylist and creator of objects for the press and publishing. After studying at the ESAG school of design in Paris, she became a freelance graphic designer before moving towards the creation of poetic and unusual objects. Author of a number of craft books, she is a jack-of-all-trades and works in many different media, including paper, lighting design, repurposing objects, sewing, photography and crochet.

ACKNOWLEDGMENTS

I am always impressed by the way some artists appropriate ordinary techniques like crochet and knitting, taking them beyond the domestic realm of crafting and breaking down the barriers of traditional creativity. Over my years of writing about art, I have been lucky enough to observe their work at close hand and I am constantly fascinated by the way they push the limits of their medium and find ways to endlessly reinvent it. It therefore seemed self-evident, even vital, to bring them all together in this book. I would like to thank all the featured artists for agreeing to take part, for the time they took to explain their artistic approaches, for the enthusiasm they demonstrated throughout the development of the project, and also for their talent, imagination and incomparable work.

I would also like to thank Céline and Christelle from the Pyramyd publishing house for their support throughout the writing of this book.

On the cover:
Shine Reclining by Jo Hamilton. Crochet, wool, 2015

Translated from the French *Ceci n'est pas un pull: Le tricot et le crochet dans l'art contemporain* by Francisca Garvie

First published in the United Kingdom in 2018 by
Thames & Hudson Ltd, 181A High Holborn, London WC1V 7QX

Original edition © 2017 Pyramyd éditions, Paris
This edition © 2018 Thames & Hudson Ltd, London

British Library Cataloguing-in-Publication Data
A catalogue record for this book is available from the British Library

ISBN 978-0-500-23988-9

Printed and bound in China

To find out about all our publications, please visit
www.thamesandhudson.com. There you can subscribe to our e-newsletter, browse or download our current catalogue, and buy any titles that are in print.